RIPTIDE
NEW WRITING FROM THE HIGHLANDS AND ISLANDS

EDITED BY
SHARON BLACKIE & DAVID KNOWLES

TWO RAVENS
PRESS

Published by Two Ravens Press Ltd
Green Willow Croft
Rhiroy
Lochbroom
Ullapool
Ross-shire IV23 2SF

www.tworavenspress.com

The right of the editors and contributors to be identified as the authors of this work has been asserted by them in accordance with the Copyright, Designs and Patent Act, 1988.
Collection © Two Ravens Press, 2007. For copyright of contributors see page 165.

ISBN: 978-1-906120-02-3

British Library Cataloguing in Publication Data: a CIP record for this book can be obtained from the British Library.

Designed and typeset by Two Ravens Press.
Cover design by David Knowles and Sharon Blackie.

Printed on Forest Stewardship Council-accredited paper by Biddles Ltd., King's Lynn, Norfolk.

Introduction

The word *anthology* derives from the Greek word for 'garland' or 'collection of flowers.' What we have in *Riptide* can perhaps then be thought of as the literary equivalent of the *Flora Celtica:* a kind of field-guide to the different species of writing that can be found today in the Highlands and Islands of Scotland. It isn't an exhaustive guide, of course. The region supports more talent than we could hope to capture in one volume. But we have here a full spectrum of top writers at their best, rubbing shoulders with some exciting newcomers.

Other than quality, there is no theme that is common to the work we selected for *Riptide*. The Highlands and Islands embrace writers of all nationalities, as well as a thriving selection of home-grown varieties. And so, naturally, the writing here is as diverse as the origins of the authors. There is writing that celebrates the beauty of the land, and writing with a rich, hardy and contemporary strand of Highland mythology running through it. There is also writing which takes a hard look at the issues of the day and of the place.

We believe that the stories and poems in this collection bring together the best of the new and the old energies that flow through this beautiful region. We hope that you find it as exciting to read as it was to bring together.

Sharon Blackie and David Knowles
Lochbroom, February 2007

Contents

Andrew Greig
That Headlong River   1
Adventures with Hoteniensis   2

Pauline Prior-Pitt
Shore Sequence   6
Stuff   9

Cynthia Rogerson
Instead of Beauty   11

John Glenday
untitled   15
The Woodcutter's Daughter   16
For Lucie   17
The Twins   18

Clio Gray
Nil Sorski and the Walrus   19

Nicky Guthrie
Resonance   25

David Ross
The Lands of Smooth Control   27

Anne Macleod
Schrödinger's Card   31

Morag Henderson
Jenny of the Pockets   38

Kevin MacNeil
Prayer, with Deaths   45

Donald S. Murray
Sandreel   47

David Knowles
Shin   52
The Language of Trains   53

Peter Urpeth
The Clearing   57
Red Kites at Docherty   64

Alison F. Napier
Flight   65
Message in a Bottle   69

Angus Dunn
Animals   73
Three Short Texts   77

John McGill
Aald Broon   79

Pam Beasant

The Anniversary 86
How long does it take to write a poem? 87
Winter Dawn 88
Land/Mind 89
Betrayal 90
Running with a Snow Leopard 91

Joanna Ramsey

The Long View 92

Elyse Jamieson

Peyton and Lewis Tailoring 102

Mandy Haggith

Dead Leaves 106
Hailstorm 107
Zen Gardener 108

Mark Ryan Smith

Harvest 109

Daibhidh Martin

Black and White Noise 113
Thievery of the Ocean 114
Tiptoe 115

Yvonne Gray

On the Ridge: Spring 2003 117
Summer Terraces 118

Alison Flett
Here He Comes								119

Morag MacInnes
Herring Bones								126
Capstan Full Strength Navy Cut				127
What Gets Said and What Gets Done			129

Robert Davidson
F111 Over Culloden							138

Eva Faber
Something Perfect In Between					139

Laureen Johnson
Mainlanded									144

Sharon Blackie
Freefall										145

Andrew Greig

That Headlong River
(for John Glenday)

That headlong river is bound for the sea.
By it you may find a links
and play a while there, knowing it
a foolish thing.

Standing over a tight lie
I hear a distant roar:
surf's up on the estuary.

It's good to be here,
knowing desire, heat and thirst
yet cooled by spray as we commit
to long shots on the inward nine.

We pray, if we do at all,
for soft hands, a steady head
to calmly stroke the last putt home

then leave the bonnie, testing course
without glancing at the scorecard
which was our fairway, not the green,
our flag but not the hole.

Adventures with Hoteniensis

What day in Eternity is this? A Monday? In any case, the eye opens, a fresh page beckons: we begin.

My first encounter with Hoteniensis was through – and do I mean through! – our family's *Encyclopaedia Britannica*. No point looking him up in your local library, should one with books in it still exist. His entry appears only in that old and profoundly obscure edition, one that I later learned had hastily been withdrawn, reason un-stated. The subsequent edition does not include him and to this day, none do.

Last week I donned stout shoes and jeans – the world may have changed temperature, sea-level, superpowers and religious outlook, but jeans remain – and walked over the bealach whose name translates as *The Pass of the Cattle,* but in that now-dead language sounds like wind over moors with a hint of crunching distant shells. From there I took the path my own feet have fashioned through the years, down into the village of Achiltibuie. There I entered what passes for a library in this, our little town – the part that is not underwater – and, calling on memories of the early C21st typed on the electro-felt, went through the *Woggle* portal in search once more of Hoteniensis.

And drew a blank. He had managed to erase himself entirely from the Pan-Asiatic Virtual Empire's hungriest search-engine! If only I could do the same.

My father's father had ordered that encyclopaedia from Edinburgh the day he retired as a shoe-maker. It came by coach, in fourteen volumes; black and sober as the family Bible, the spine's lettering boldly gold. He believed in God, my unmet grandfather William Burness, late emissary of the C19th, rather as we once believed in CCTV in the early C21st: a regrettable necessity that protected public order at the cost of increased private disturbance. But let that rest, along with other vanished calamities! Climb down from that pulpit in your mind; rejoin the congregation of churchless kirk of Storrey!

Now my paternal grandfather William, at whose black-suited patriarchal feet – but did I mention he played the euphonium? No? Our natty paterfamilias, parping those melodious bass farts with the Town Band at the Curling Club Annual Winter Gala, cannot have been entirely without humour or rough poetry.

2

He also keenly followed the fortunes of the MCC in the Antipodean Colonies, by telegraph – despite never playing the game, which suggests a man possessed of both industry and a sense of the truly ridiculous. I mean, the importance of unimportant things. (It cannot be without significance that the only man to win the Nobel Prize for Literature *and* appear in *Wisden* was Sam Beckett! A fellow euphoniumist, I believe, though *Woggle* remains obstinately silent on the subject.)

Yet it is at those black leather brogues that grandfather William painstakingly stitched for himself in the lamp-lit evenings while his dear wife read to him – haltingly, for her eyesight was poor, the gas mantle of as dubious quality as had been her education of the doings of Arbroath and the world – I say at those surprisingly neat little feet poking out on the ice in the only photo remaining of him in the world, at the North Angus Curling Clubs Bonspiel – it's at those feet, with their stamina for self-improvement, financial caution and musical alarums, that the fault or credit must be laid.

For that first meeting with Hoteniensis.

For this story that, despite my anecdotage, has already begun.

I tell it, of course, for the pleasure of talking here in the body of the kirk of Storrey, the only parish in which I still feel at home. I tell it to keep my final silence at bay for one more day. (Is it Sunday? Does it matter? Does anything, apart from *Him?*)

Above all, I will tell it for Eve, offspring of my last secret, in the hope that she will visit once again.

My grandfather took delivery of that uncanny edition – whose compositors in Edinburgh were already resetting type over an inexplicable incursion into their leaden universe – off the morning coach from Brechin, and staggered with it in his arms down the mud street to his door, which he kicked gently with his dainty foot till his dear wife opened up.

'It's arrived!' he murmured as he lurched indoors. 'In here is the kenning of everything there is that can be kenned, from Tignabruich to Timbuktu! To distant heck with the euphonium! Fetch Andra and wee Donald!'

Andrew and wee Donald – my uncle and father as laddies – came running barefoot from what they cried *a gemme o toolies*, meaning playing marbles, to attend the opening of the crates, and see the great tomes hefted in their father's skeely hands. My father (wee Donald) at the end of his days would lower his long neb into the whisky glass, sniff and murmur, 'No a patch on the whiff o' yon encyclopaedia'.

I know Eve – would that she were here again! – would roll those fine grey lustrous eyes, and murmur *Get on with it*. And I am, I will, I shall.

Yes, I am working my way to Hoteniensis rather circumspectly, a little frightened to re-open the emotional file on those days again. Impossible not to see my then-lover clothes-free on the bed one hot June afternoon, laid out like a peeled willow wand, so supple and pliant and singing the flesh as she murmurs *Get on with it, man …*

Let us concentrate today on what was given, rather than what has been taken away.

When I hefted down the massive volume of my father's father that night all those years ago, who knows what I was looking for? One might brood on the life we stumble through en route to the life we were really after … but no. To hell with elegy and clergy, both overly prevalent in these times! Hence, vain speculation!

I was on my knees in the early years of the C21st, turning foxed pages in a dead house, looking for whatever one looks for when there is nothing left on television, when the flesh is tired and hope is lost. I was looking to avoid myself, as we do, while yearning to connect once more. As we do. In a dwam I glanced through 'Hottentots,' then idly flicked back a few pages, and there it was:

Hoteniensis 'the reprehensible' – a Berber healer of the Rif and High Atlas mountains. It is not possible to grasp, by reading, the force of his teachings.

And here is a small map, indicating his hinterland. It looks like mountain drylands. So many bare peaks and only one small, clear river. It is by that burn that I kneel, trying to scoop up water through split fingers. The water runs through before I can get it to my mouth.

When I look up at the thudding sound – which may be my own heart, or another's – *He* is there.

Hoteniensis. That is his name today; he could have others. Short, wide, muscular, unshaved. His cloak is travel-stained, his head is unusually large, his hair matted and dusty. I would rise but his great hands grip my shoulders. I shake at the force of his grip. To stare into his eyes – his offer no choice in the matter – is to be shoved off the mind's highest cliff.

Bear, bull, barrel-chested Minotaur man, he grips me and stares down into my eyes. His mouth opens, the great lips part and curl; his breath is scorching but oddly honeyed as he rumbles into my face:

Will you be alive tomorrow?

'I can't know that!' I gasp. His stained and ragged teeth clash as he retorts:

And if you're not, I will say it was inevitable!

He roars with laughter as he shakes me. Yes, I've got it. Great teaching, thanks. Now let me go.

Because that's how things are. He grasps me closer, forces his body against mine. It seems we are wrestling by the river and I am falling back. This is not rape; it is not precisely my body that he is overthrowing. I am falling and he is on top, pinning me down. A triumphant shout as he kneels on my right shoulder.

It yields, it cracks.

He kneels on my left shoulder. It too cracks.

Something is broken.

I am a stick cracked across his knee. Some tense matter has been broken; it's a relief, like dying. It may in fact be dying.

But it has only begun, the forceful teaching of Hoteniensis. He forces his head against mine. His great head, his stubble coarse as steel wool. His breath scorches my cheek. The pressing is unbearable.

Then he starts to whisper in my ears. His voice sounds like scree on the Great Stone Chute on Sgurr Alasdair on the Cuillin, being run down by a god into the gleaming Sound of Raasay.

At that sound, all the cells of my body start unravelling. All thoughts, all Reason, start to crash. It's an internal landslide with no known end. 'I didn't know, I didn't know – ' I cry.

Well, you ken noo!

I couldn't know they would be so physical, these adventures with Hoteniensis that had only just begun.

The evening sky is silting up over the bealach. I do not think my grey-eyed Eve will come today.

Perhaps it is Monday after all.

Pauline Prior-Pitt

Shore Sequence
Traigh Iar Sollas 2006

January 26

bent into the wind
against sand blow
high tide
gnaws the dunes

January 30

low sun on low water
my long shadow
walks into a pink blue sky
and dune gold wet reflection
waves in a hurry
fling diamonds at my feet

February 5

sea in the sky
sky in the sea
clouds foam in the wet stretch

February 26

the sea sleeps placed
underneath a blue silk cloth
soft sighs sink into the sand

March 1

you're out in it
definitely out in it
snow bowling across the sand,
grey clouds bulging with it
splitting with it pelting with it
dark green water
between grey and white

March 2
Early morning

brighter than the brightest
lighter than the lightest
palest pale pink sky
stillest still blue milk sea

Late morning

bright white hills
lazy indigo sea

April 6

Look at you
flouncing your white petticoats
onto the shore
grabbing pebbles as you dance away

Pauline Prior-Pitt

April 10

sand spattered with rain
like rough paper

May 3

today the sea has left skeins
of treasure on the sand
each wave ebbs a necklace
seaweed threads, broken shells, feathers, straw and fine peat
   grains

Stuff

They don't like it
when their old bedroom
becomes the spare room

when you ask them to remove their stuff
and they say
what stuff
and you say
that stuff in the chest of drawers
stuff in the wardrobe
stuff in boxes under the bed

and they say
oh that stuff
there isn't room in my flat for that stuff

and you say
it has to go
and will they come and sort it
take what they want and you'll get rid of the rest
and they say
yes they'll come

and they come
but they don't sort it or take it
and it stays

and you offer to sort it for them
but they say
no they'll sort it
and it stays

until the day comes when
you empty the stuff in the drawers
and the wardrobe
into black plastic sacks
and put them in the hall
by the front door
with the boxes from under the bed
ready for them to collect
but they don't collect

and you move the sacks and boxes into the garage
out of the house
and it's a squeeze to park the car
but they're out of the house

And by the time they come and take them away
if ever they do
other boxes are under the spare bed
boxes of toys
for their children to play with
when they come to stay.

Cynthia Rogerson

Instead of Beauty

After she gives up on love, Addie decides that all she really wants is a baby. A baby! A tiny person to carry around and cook lovely cakes for; someone who'll never look at her as if she's nobody. She is hung-over; exhausted and taut. Outside, the July rain is un-dramatic, self-effacing, as if it knows that its timing is bad. Her kitchen is humid and her head aches. A fragile day altogether, requiring great care and strength of will; and it is also the saddest time of the day: three in the afternoon. She considers her options carefully. She has nearly run out of men – Lochinellie has a certain number and no more. By the time she makes and drinks her cup of bitter black coffee, she has a shortlist of one. Down to the bottom of the barrel now, no mistake.

Joe Forbes, the fish man.

He is the only one with no prying family in the area, no wedding ring, and no obvious defects – if you didn't count his probable virginity as a defect. Or his perennial stink of fish, his ugliness (though his shoulders are quite nice) and his complete lack of conversation. He is the most silent, ugly and alone man she has ever met. Though, now she thinks of it, Joe is curiously un-lonely looking.

'So, Joe!' she says to him that night at the bar in the hotel. (Addie never wastes time, and she knew she'd find him here. Single men in Lochinellie gravitate to the bar at dusk, like single men everywhere in the Highlands, like thirsty beasts to the watering hole.) 'What you drinking, Joe?'

She buys them both a pint, then lets him buy her two more. They sit in silence for an hour, and then she tells him that she wants a baby from him.

'What do you think? You like me, right?' she asks, her voice hard as hailstones; hard as desperation. Her face all rosy and her eyes excited. She could be uncannily pretty at this time of night, for about half an hour. Before time was called and the lights came full on again. As if her much younger, untroubled self resurfaced in some alcohol-fuelled twilight, in order to seduce. A spirit siren on a mission.

'I've seen you looking, and it's not as if you've got a queue of women knocking on your door, Joe. Is it? I know you like me.'

'Of course I ... like you. What's ... not to like? You're ... fun. But, Addie – that's hardly the point.'

This is the longest sentence she's ever heard him say. He says the words in a halting staccato, as if English is his third language. There's a sheen of sweat on his nose.

'Aw, come on: of course it's the point. If you didn't like me, at least a little, then we'd never manage it at all. I'd say that you liking me was the entire bloody point, for you. You'd get a bit of experience; I'd get my baby.'

Pause, while she searches unsuccessfully for eye contact.

'I'd not be wanting any money off you. Ever. You'd be well clear of it all, really. All the advantages; none of the hassle.'

Again she waits for his response, but he just looks emptily at her as if his whole stock of words has gone. She stops waiting, satisfied that his muteness is entirely appropriate, given who he is and what she is asking. She leans forward and whispers: 'I'm only wanting your sperm. And just for one night, when the time is right for me. For making a baby. There's really only a few days a month it'll work. And it's only you I'm asking. I thought about it, and you're the only one. The best one for the job. The best man.'

Joe takes a long pull of his beer and shifts in his seat. This feels like words to Addie.

'It'll just take a few minutes, actually, Joe. No need for staying the night, even. Unless you want to, of course. You might fall asleep, and then I'd just let you sleep.'

'No!' It bursts out of him with such finality that she lurches forward, already grieving for this sweet fish-smelling baby. She has trouble breathing naturally, and her voice acquires an unattractive whine.

'But why? What're you afraid of? It'll not hurt. I'll be dead gentle.'

She puts her hand on his, which feels oily and rough, but she doesn't remove it. She is surprised how easy it is to ignore the oily stickiness, but Lord – he stinks of fish. There'd be no getting rid of that smell.

'Please, Joe. Just consider it.'

'It's ... wrong.'

'How can it be wrong? Everyone – but you, that is – does it all the time! It's the strongest instinct there is, to make babies. Love is all crap.

12

It's just a trick of nature to make sure the human race doesn't die out.'
Joe shrugs, finishes his pint.
'Ach, you'll be sorry. I'm great, so I am. Ask anyone.'
He looks round the pub. It's true; almost all the men drinking could probably vouch for Addie's skills. He sighs, and his sigh has longing and sadness in it. Then something happens to the room and everyone in it, and though things look the same, they are not. In fact, unseen by the customers, the barmaid has opened the back door and a surfeit of oxygenated sea air has entered the bar. Addie removes her hand from Joe's hand, and instantly he misses it. He misses it like he'd miss his own hand. He buys another round, then they sit in silence for seven minutes and drink in rhythm, each raising their pint glass and drinking at the same time. They look at the bottles behind the bar and there is a pleasant stillness to their silence, as if the new air has induced a truce.

Joe is a word miser, and in any case, she is a lousy listener. But her muscles have wisdom and memories and don't require language. She puts her hand back in his hand, leaves it there until he wraps his fingers around it.

'Listen, I know it's a lot to ask. I'm not daft.' She doesn't look at him or the bottles now, but looks out of the window. The sea is visible in the white lines of breaking waves. It is raining, of course: that same thin seemingly-English drizzle, with no real force behind it. She has a sudden wish for the rain to really rain, to stop holding back. She wishes for a screaming hurricane of wind and rain, to make all choice irrelevant, to obliterate the hotel and everyone in it. She sighs and her sigh has tears of frustration in it.

'Shit, Joe. I just want a baby. It's all I can think of. I've given up on the other stuff.'

Joe nods sympathetically, excuses himself to use the toilet, and when he returns, asks if she's all right to see herself home. She says yes, and he leaves her sitting there, feeling strange, with her half-empty glass of flat beer and the insipid rain.

One day, a few weeks later, Joe spots Addie standing alone by the quay in the torrential rain without a jacket. She is so strange! Looking at the sea and sky, which the rain has joined in a seamless tableau of depressing summer. It's been a menopausal summer altogether: too hot and then too cold; moody and intense. When she begins to turn in his direction

13

he quickly turns as well, and walks briskly away.

Three weeks later, early in the morning, the sun remembers its own point and sizzles. The light explodes over Lochinellie like a luminous blessing, and nothing looks dull or ordinary. Not even the rusty petrol pumps. Not even the Co-op sign with the missing letters. The whole place steams away, and Addie pulls on her favourite dress – red cotton with tiny white stars. She bounds down the road to Joe's cottage, enjoying the air on her skin, and thinks what an extraordinarily fine thing it is, some days, to be above the ground and not in it. Joe is walking to his lorry, all muffled up in a fleece as if he hasn't really noticed the day yet.

'Joe!'

He greets her by tilting his head and smiling, closed-mouthed.

'Joe! What a fine day!'

He makes a noise of assent, then opens the door to his lorry and swings one leg up. She tells him that this is the day they can make a baby.

'It's the best day, Joe. What time are you back tonight?'

He freezes, half-way into the cab. 'I'll be gone for three days.' He pulls himself the rest of the way in and shuts his door. Starts up the engine. Sudden glimpse of Addie in her faded red-and-white dress and anxious pale face, lips red as if she's been nibbling them, and a halo from the sun. He salutes her goodbye, and while he checks his rear-view mirror she swings open the passenger door and heaves herself in. He stares at her, but she keeps her face forward, and is so still that it is as if she is willing herself into invisibility. He pauses for a moment, then pulls out into the road. She looks out of the window at the boats in the harbour; notices how they never rock the same way and the masts are always at odds. Then Joe shifts down to make the steep brae out of Lochinellie.

An hour later, after the sun slinks away in another huff, he offers her his jumper. She pulls it on. It's rough against her skin and way too big, but there is a sense of relief in the roughness and bigness. She feels safe. They are still not looking at each other, as if there is danger in acknowledgment.

'Thank you, Joe,' she whispers, soft as Marilyn Monroe, soft as astonishment. 'I was freezing.' After a minute she lays her hand on his knee, and she keeps it there all the way to Carlisle. Like a piece of luck, or unexpected sun on an overcast day.

John Glenday

and the word lost for a single breath, as I lie against you; I promise everything that ever was will grow alive again: look where the line of Moses arches towards Egypt; swaying reeds in green shallows; my hands on you like the rain in barley; a ship skews and tilts from a mountaintop into the flood; the first man in his sudden ignorance spits a sour apple whole again, turns to her, who will be no more than an ache in the bones of his heart, as you are for me; for this breath, in my arms, the rain falling through the moment's light; then let me rest for one day, for the strength to unmake myself; the beasts of the earth and the great whales, to shift continents into oceans, to take down the firmament and blink into the failing light, the failing darkness for a moment's breath, a moment's touch, brushing your heart like this, as all things fall back into themselves, leaving nothing in the beginning but the word

The Woodcutter's Daughter

Once upon a time there was a great forest that shelved into the distant haze like a blue-green ocean. In the heart of the forest lived a poor woodcutter and his daughter. There was no larger forest in all the kingdom, and there would never be an end to his work. Every morning the woodcutter would test the gleam of his axe then set off into the stillness by the one path allowed him. Each evening he would return, tired and hungry. His daughter would set his bowl before him, watch him from the corner as he ate, and clear the table after him, singing quietly to the shadows and herself. Nothing of the world outside intruded. No-one passed by and they saw nothing of the further world – only the fretwork of sky through the high pines; cloudlets fraying and reforming; gentle tatters of birdsong and rain. One day the woodcutter's daughter felt an unusual pain in her breast, and because she knew what it was – or perhaps because she did not – she wove trails of woodrush into something that could have been a toy boat, with a twig for a mast and a sycamore leaf for a sail and for cargo she cut a small cloth purse from her apron, and ate the flesh clean from a blood-black cherry and closed the cherrystone in the purse she had made. She bound it with a single strand of her hair and placed it in the woven boat, tied a cord to the boat's mast and hung it from a branch of an old beech tree in the clearing. Then she went back to her work, singing quietly to herself until the pain in her heart was bearable. One day, she knew, some terrible wind would rise up and blow through the heart of the forest. It would rattle the shingles and scour at the window panes and scatter the wood-smoke from the chimney and rush off through the branches with a sound like the sound of the ocean over stones, and the little boat would dip and luff and veer as if anchored in a windswept harbour. The woodcutter's daughter imagined how she would watch in astonishment as it moved, knowing she need only reach up and cut the cord for it to sail off through the trees and never stop until it had beached itself where the forest came to an end and something else began.

John Glenday

For Lucie

born 5 December 2005

Born at the deepest sounding of the year,
how apt it was that we named you
for the light: no more

than a small light, mind – a spunk; a spill;
a stub of tallow cradled against the draft;
while our twinned shadows angle

and fall away behind, lengthening into the past.
You are our toast of brightness.
Here's to you, then, and to us,

to your world and to ours.
We raise you towards the dark.
May you make of it something else.

John Glenday

The Twins

for Sophie and Cameron Neville

How typical. Given your pick
of seven thousand stars, in all their
strange, familiar scaffoldings,

you had to choose the simplest:
two flecks of Knoydart mica, shivering
between Munlochy and the Firth.

How long ago and insulate
and frail they seemed – like God
and the shadow of his absence
in our lives:

helplessly adrift between
the dusk and dark and dusk;
but always together,
and sailing together over everything.

Clio Gray

Nil Sorski and the Walrus

I'm in the pillory at Cholmogory having just had my ears sliced off.
We are one month into winter, thank God, so the cold has numbed
the pain. Even the English rope-traders, who founded the town and run
the courts according to their own rules, are not so cruel as to find you
thieving in summer. All trials are put off till the first snows – at least
when the ear-chopping sentence is the likely result, as it always is when
found guilty of theft. It would be a different story if you got caught by
the walrus-hunters who live up on the coast. They'd ask no leave; just
string you over some thorn bush in the swamp and leave you to the
mosquitoes. Mercy is not something they're familiar with, either at work
or with friends, let alone strangers. At least we get to keep our feet on the
ground, even if most of the year it's frozen. The hunters though, they
take off onto the White Sea and up the Kola coast any time the water's
clear. They'll damp up at first fog and never dry out till journey's end,
which might be months. They get stuck in ice-floes, flipped by whales
and wind, drowned, starved or just plain frozen to death, most of which
they could have done without leaving home. Then there's the walrus:
fifteen feet of fury hanging from your gaff, your bones vibrating with
their bellows, their mouths waiting to snap you like a seal, your fingers
shivering on the harpoon hoping you'll hit just right and not make them
angrier than they already are. You want to get them well dead before you
hack off their tusks and use their intestines to make raincoats. Knee-high
in blubber and blood, tearing at the skin, hacking through the muscle.
Slicing up the gut is bloody hard work – I know, I've tried it – and slitting
the stomach pure stinks. But if you're lucky, it's full of cardium-cockles
and then you've made a fortune – they love them on the dining tables
of Moscow. No such luck for me. I lasted barely a month before I had
to be put ashore at Gremikha, sick as a man can be without dying. I
spent the rest of the season boiling tusks up with vinegar and unrolling
them – which is still hard work if not bloody, and makes your fingers
look like boiled cabbage. But at least you kept your feet on the ground

and the food in your belly stayed there. And I learned something else, apart from the reek and rip of it all – they don't have ears, those walrus. Or if they do, they're hidden somewhere on the inside.

Someone is lifting my head, sending a pink icicle shivering into my beard.

'Okay, Sylvester, time to go.'

It's Bernard. He removes the bolt-pins and lifts the beam from my neck and wrists. I'm frozen stiff as the pillory-pole and stay in position: arms in front of me slacked at the elbows; neck craned forward, the top of my back a bell-curve – the pillory having been built for shorter men than me. Bernard throws me over his shoulder, a shape into which I am perfectly bent, and carts me off to our cabin to wrap me in sealskins and fill me with vodka-laced borscht.

'Not too bad, then?' It's Bernard again. I've thawed out a little, but am still bowed in front of the fire, my head bleeding into a straw-stuffed cushion. He's obviously shouting from the exaggerated way he's moving his mouth, and through the scabs and the bandages I can just make out the words. Or maybe I read them. Either way, I try to sit up, but keep losing my balance and have to lie down again. I know that this will pass: like sea-sickness, my legs will learn to adjust and I'll soon be up on my feet. After a slicing, you're allowed a week or two before you're back to the factory, jute-dust everywhere: in your nose and hair and clothes and eyes. We wear goggles, like the Lapps showed us, with crosses instead of slits to protect our eyes, but that dust gets everywhere no matter how hard you try. Still, no doubting the goggles are useful against the glare of the snow, and they're free, courtesy of the management. They're not all bad, those English. Been settled here for hundreds of years and you'd only know they're English because they drink beer before their vodka. That's something we Prussians appreciate – Old Country habits die hard – plus they stick to themselves and don't interfere. A place like this, you don't want people poking at you with questions about this or that. You come for a reason, or like me, you get sent and nobody wants to talk about that.

It's Nil Sorski's Eve – he's the patron saint of the *skit* at the end of the village. The monks came from the big monastery at Beloozero years ago and though there's only eleven left, they own a lot of land, which is bizarre considering their patron was known as Nil the Non-Possessor and got into trouble for claiming all monks should be poor. They also make a radish liqueur that men have killed for, and on the Eve of Nil Sorski those who've done them well during the past twelve months each get a couple of bottles. It's blackmail, obviously: but it works, and for those who get given, it's the biggest night of the year.

Bernard had to re-sump their cess-pit back in June when the thaw threatened to sink their radish-plots and the entire crop along with it. One big favour deserves another, and we've got a crate of the stuff and beggars have been hammering at the door all day. Bernard took precautions and strengthened the bolts whilst I dug the dirt up under the fire – the only place the earth's loose – and buried most of the cache for later use. We've also put several in the eaves for the coming week, though out of drunken reach in case we get thirstier tonight than we ought, or visitors get violent.

In honour of Nil Sorski the Non-Possessor we hand over our goods to each other, a gesture of great trust in this climate of cold and starvation. Bernard has given me a bottle containing my two ears. I am so touched that I almost weep. He must have fought the wild dogs to get them, and beaten off that blasted woman who makes unguents out of anything she can get her hands on. Human parts are especially powerful – or so she tells anyone that will listen. When someone goes off into the forest to hunt elk or bear, they always take vodka to keep them warmed up. And she's always there when they return in case they got too drunk and fell asleep in the snow and got frostbite. She'll go round after them scraping up the blackened bits the second they've fallen off. Some would say that it's a harmless hobby, and that's she's only cleaning up what others don't want, but when she tries to sell you some disgusting black-green poultice, you have to wonder how many hunters' fingers and toes have gone into the mix.

It's with such thoughts in mind that I gaze gratefully at my bottled ears. The lump in my throat stops me speaking, so I pat Bernard on the back and, wobbling to my feet with the aid of a stick, go to get my gift for him. I take my special jar from below my bed and hand it over. It is half-filled with sugar gems the size of gooseberries. They are webbed all over with gold-leaf and coloured the brightest crocus yellow you've ever seen. The sherbet fizz and tang of lemon hide the treasure within – a sunflower seed carved in the profile of the Emperor, the Blessed Bonaparte. We take one each and suck it with reverence, removing the seed and laying it carefully to dry upon the hearth. Time was, we had to swallow them so our allegiance would remain unknown, but nobody cares, not now, not here. Still, it's a secret pleasure we'll not share with anyone else. They remind us of our glory days when we were young and strong.

For over fifteen years I've carried that jar, a talisman of my faith and my adopted country. I thought The Corsican would save Europe; I spied for him at Austerlitz, paraded my Prussian papers, fought for the Austrians, allied myself to Alexander, fed false information to the Russian generals. We went from strength to strength. I fought with Bonaparte through Krasnoi and Smolensk and then, at Borodino, we hatched a plan and once again I was enlisted as a spy. I borrowed the uniform of a deceased officer and withdrew with the defeated Russian troops. I would glean what intelligence I could about what Commander-in-Chief Kutusov planned to do next. I would sow dissent and dis-ease amongst the ranks, and then I would desert and join my own army back on the banks of the Niemen. If I hadn't got accidentally shot by a boy who'd got head-fever and gone mad, all would have been well. However, when Bernard dragged me onto the hospital cart and I declared myself Brigade Leader Lyubivich number 53024, my rank was hotly disputed by a fellow patient who claimed to know that I was no such thing. It was a bad moment, and was only resolved when I punched the patient hard in the head, whereupon he died. A court-martial followed, with the result that I was convicted for stealing a senior officer's uniform – apparently my fellow patient would have been dead within the week even without my intervention, so the murder charge was dropped. I chose exile over imprisonment and, as Bernard frequently reminds me, we should count ourselves lucky that the military were in such disarray and the court proceedings shabby and unenthusiastic. Or we would certainly have been discovered as the spies we were. He's right, of course; he's always been the better man than me.

I hand him over the jar. It was the one thing, apart from Bernard, that I was allowed to take with me into exile. Just a bag of lemon-drops, the Russians were told, to help me with the cold. Had they known what they really were – symbol of Empire and their defeat – I'd have been long buried, my head somewhere separate from my feet.

Bernard cradles the jar upon his knees, his eyes shining in their reflected glow. We pour another drink and clink our glasses, toast our faith and freedom. I tell him again to be careful with those sweets – only one every now and then. The startling colour comes from Acid of Picric, and though stunning to see and marvellous to taste, it has the slight disadvantage of being poisonous. More so than arsenic, I am told, and I add the story – possibly apocryphal – of Ludwig, King of Bavaria who almost killed his entire court by creating confectionery canaries in cages of spun sugar. These replaced the real ones, two hours earlier singing their heads off and now spitted arse-to-beak upon the fire. He might have been mad, but one doubts that there was murder on his mind. Although, of course, it could have been the chef. They could make you eat yesterday's stockings if they're good enough at their job; make the worst ingredients taste good. One can imagine a building up of bitterness if they're not appreciated for what they do. A bit like spies. Although one assumes that most cooks don't become murderers.

I, on the other hand, have already removed a small handful of my golden sweets. I have placed them in a leather pouch and posted them through the door of Patrovich Davidov. He is a mean and greedy man who drinks two cups of vodka before breakfast, and who lost his wife to a man who digs holes for a living. Any kind of hole will do, and hard work though it is to dig in our soil, it's hardly the height of social climbing. And yet this Patrovich Davidov, the sole accuser at my trial, was believed above me because he works in the courthouse and I only graft in the factory. What use would I have for Councillor Rostov's pocket watch, Bernard (as my defence lawyer) demanded of the judge? We all know it stops in the autumn and doesn't start again till spring. That I *did* have a use for it is none of anyone's business but my own. It made a fine pair of earrings for Valda – whose services, as even Davidov knows, don't come cheap.

Ah well. What's done is done. Bernard has poured me another drink and the fire is finally warming my bones. I can hardly hear the constant beggars battering at the door; shortly we will have to let them in before they get out the ice-picks. And, thanks to Bernard, my ears are safe upon the shelf. I am told that my hearing will recover – there's quite a few round about who've had the thieves' verdict passed upon them – so once again I will have the pleasure of hearing the swans fly low in spring, and pretend to understand Bernard's obscure jokes. Valda is used to those of us lacking in such appendages and anyway, she says that she means to retire. I have saved enough silver to fashion a ring, and thank God once again for His blessing. God bless France, which I once believed would give the world the liberty and equality it still needs. God bless Bernard for being a sage friend and saver of ears. God bless Napoleon and those who made gilded sherbets in his image. God Bless St Sorski and all the seraphim for this night of gifts. And Davidov will find his, I have no doubt; and being a greedy man and without friends or wife, he will no doubt consume the entire golden hoard himself and gain his just desserts. Thank you, Rostov, for your watch. Because of you I have lost my ears, but Valda has a fine present for her retirement, most of which I do not doubt she will spend with me. And, like the walrus, I will do most of my listening on the inside.

Nicky Guthrie

Resonance

'Go by yourself when you're under no pressure for time, and spend as long as you need. Think about what you would like to have, choose five things and make a note of them. I'll do the same. We won't look at the value of anything till we've made our choices. If there are things we both want, we'll either toss a coin or, if that happens more than once, divide them equally. Everything left we'd better auction or sell.'

'Okay,' I said. 'When are you going?'

'I went yesterday.'

Two months since our parents died and the world goes on just the same, as I always knew, in theory, that it would.

I have already disposed of their clothes, shoes, toothbrushes, perishables in the kitchen. Most of the clothes went to Oxfam, some of Dad's to the recycling centre. As I thrust my mother's pink sheepskin slippers into a bin-bag I did feel that perhaps I ought to keep them so that I could put my hand inside and feel where her toes had been and get all emotional. But they were empty.

Now I sit at my mother's dressing table and wrap my fingers around the cool ivory handle of her hairbrush, deliberately placing my hand over the exact space where her hand would have been. I hold the brush up and look for her hairs, any little motes of dandruff, but as I could have predicted, it is clean. I lift it to my face and bury my nose in the natural bristles. The tang of ammonia rushes her to me and I love the horrible smell.

The back of the brush is inlaid with the initials J.J.G. Jennifer Jane Groves. My great-grandmother. She is in the hairbrush too, but much, much more faintly than my mother.

I place the brush back beside its matching hand-mirror and reach behind the dressing-table to heave up the window. She always kept her room full of fresh, chilly air, with a hint of clean linen.

I look out on her view, watch a breeze rustle through the trees and a solitary crow bark its way over the house.

I go downstairs to my father's bedroom and enter without knocking. The dense smell of stale air and Dettol clings to me like cobwebs as I take up position in the centre, tense. His presence and his absence are fighting for position. His snores drip angrily down the walls, leaving a sticky smear that you can almost see. His desk will be quite valuable, and his glass-fronted bookshelf. Daniel can have them. They echo of his hissing, hand-rubbing tantrums that we all knew about.

Poor Dad, so lonely and isolated.

There are two dining-room tables in the dining room. And Mum's desk. She is definitely in her desk, mingled with her mother, from whom she inherited it. But the desk will be all right. If Daniel doesn't want it, somebody will pay a lot of money for it and cherish its presence. A piece of furniture can stand up for itself. Retain the characters that have gone into it. Welcoming hall chests, elegant tall-boys, pretentious drinks-cabinets, functional bedside-tables, sinister chests-of-drawers, threatening wardrobes. You know what I mean.

Smaller items are more vulnerable and need special care. Like this painting. A river with three trees on the far bank and a dead tree on the near bank. Painted by Auntie in her nineties. Almost certainly of no value, but it holds the wood-smoke smell of my grandparents' house and the sense of security that surrounded my mother. It must not be sent to the auction room where its charge would rub off on unsuspecting members of the general public. Wasted.

I step out of the French windows into the garden. The grass needs cutting and the bird-feeders are empty. CDs free from the Sunday papers glitter on strings over the broccoli and cabbages. A blackbird tugs a worm out of the grass and it snaps in two.

I am splitting, tendrils of grief escaping back to the house, searching for my mother in the bricks and mortar.

The hairbrush, the mirror that goes with it, and old Auntie's painting. Please.

David Ross

The Lands of Smooth Control

In the lands of smooth control
    nothing happens
           accidentally.
    There are no coincidences here.

In the lands of smooth control
    everything is appropriate.
    Nothing is out of place
    and there is no limit on time.

In the lands of smooth control
    the whole and the elements
    can be perceived simultaneously.

In the lands of smooth control
    events
        are predetermined.

In the lands of smooth control
    traumatic possibilities
           have been eliminated.
    There will be no prophetic illuminations
    and there will be no dance with madness.

In the lands of smooth control
    the course of any voyage
    is mapped in advance.
    (Dosages are moderate and minutely precalculated.)

David Ross

In the lands of smooth control
      there are no extremes.
      The level is uniform.
      The luminosity is constant.

In the lands of smooth control
      a limit
            has been set.

In the lands of smooth control
      objects are kept carefully inanimate
      and remain in their assigned places.
      They cooperate smoothly
      and invite attention.
                  (They do not demand it.)

In the lands of smooth control
      objects do not terrify in their brilliance.
      They permit focused investigation
      and continually allude to their final secret.

In the lands of smooth control
      this ultimate discovery
      is permitted.

But in the lands of smooth control
      one is content
            not to know.

In the lands of smooth control
      the metal is aluminium.
      Power is nuclear
      and travel is illusory.
                 (There is no smoke.)

In the lands of smooth control
     the music is the jester's music.
     Every parody suggests the same elusive theme
     but never states it.

In the lands of smooth control
     the orators are lucid.
     The philosophy is relativity
     and time has an infinite extension.
     (The ability to wait is fundamental.)

In the lands of smooth control
     poets calculate
          its area.

In the lands of smooth control
     language
          presents few difficulties.

In the lands of smooth control
     repetition is important.

In the lands of smooth control
     this name is not used.

In the lands of smooth control
     expression
          is almost exact.

In the lands of smooth control
     food is bought, meals are cooked and pans are cleaned.
     Furniture is dusted, clothes are washed
          and carpets are swept.

David Ross

Coffee is served, cigarettes are smoked
and stray animals are fed.

In the lands of smooth control
rituals are performed
religiously.
(Insurance is possible.)

In the lands of smooth control
the last puzzle
is almost solved.
The last mystery
is almost unveiled.

In the lands of smooth control
everything
is almost tangible.
The situation
is almost
grasped.

Anne Macleod

Schrödinger's Card

Everybody – even the most rational of us – needs a bit of magic in their day. My mother used to say that sea and sky and air were wrapped round harder earth, kept there by a spell. Newton might call that gravity, but my mother knew better. What Einstein and Feynman struggled to convey, she experienced in breath, in life.

Why is the sky dark at night?

Because the universe expands so fast shifting starlight cannot fill the void.

Did Olbers say that? Or did he merely put the question? No matter; my mother had her own answer: the sky is dark, she said, to let us sleep. Endless light, endless warmth are not natural; just as life lived without pain would not be life but something other. Less magic.

And when you think about it, starlight is amazing. All that energy not focused here on earth. Energy disseminated, glorious. No thin torch-beams, but pure light catapulting endless space – like hope – brightening all it touches.

My mother was strong on hope.

I saw a picture in a newspaper today of a young girl by a window reading a letter or, at least, holding a sheet of paper in her hand and looking vaguely towards it, or past it, while the carefully-arranged light offered a profile of great beauty. Her hair was a knot of curls cascading from her crown. Her skin was pale, translucent as moonlight. She held our gaze, the room behind her almost bare – an unvarnished shelf with speakers, no pictures. No mirrors. Nothing but bare wall, unpapered. Between us and her, in the foreground, a chubby, well-fed infant lay perfectly still beneath hand-knitted blankets. The child gazed at the mother, as we did, as if wondering what she could be spending so long on, what could be drawing her attention.

My mother would have said, 'It's a letter from her lover. He's coming home at last, after months, perhaps years, away.' Or 'The baby's adopted. She's holding in her hands the final papers.' Or 'An aunt has died and left her a fortune.' Or 'She can't believe it, the publishers have accepted her novel.' Or 'It's her bill from the club; all her Christmas shopping finished and paid for.'

Never in a million years would she have translated the picture to this, the photographer's title: *A girl reads the notice of eviction.*

The girl's stillness implied something important. There was no doubt of that – no doubt at all – but nothing in the moment arranged before us tendered such a bleak conclusion.

My mother would have denounced that title as false; flawed narrative. And story was indeed all it was, the moment rehearsed and set up like an old Dutch painting, an instance of light, not darkness.

Or perhaps the acting was wrong: at any rate the offered emotion felt arranged, not true. Manipulative. Undermined your pleasure in the photograph, as I must suppose it was designed to do. *What you see is not what you get.* I imagine the photographer thought it an important lesson. *Bad things happen, even to the beautiful.*

Or perhaps what he was saying was *don't read letters.* Don't *read.*

My mother supervised my reading. Taught me all I needed to know. Cards played a prominent role. She made me work at school as well, and actually the cards helped there. I was card-reader for the class, interpreting the future for any and all who sought my advice. Easy. The future was written on their foreheads. I could have told it without the cards, though they gave my friends something to focus on, somewhere to pin their eyes while hands sweated and hearts raced.

Six cards for the present. Six more for the future. It was always that first future card that caused most anxiety. Don't ask me why. I tell it like it is, that's all.

Some people worry about the future. Others worry more about those who try to read it. My mother, however, knew how to silence unbelievers and passed the trick to me. I had to resurrect it the day April Stevens, almost the cleverest girl in our year, decided to mount a rational challenge to what seemed to her an irritating game.

April was in most of my classes but we never sat together, never shared a lunch-table, not till the week after the sixth year exams. April had coined herself a busy timetable, was aiming for Oxford. Or St Andrews. She'd been muttering dissent as I laid out future hopes for a couple of our school friends. This was nothing new. I finished the readings, laid my cards aside, reaching for my sandwich.

'Well?'

'Well what?' I did not have to look up to measure the voice.

'Isn't it about time?'

I raised my eyebrows. 'Time for what?'

'You're the fortune cookie. You tell me. '

Patient by nature, I waited. April couldn't bear the silence.

'Time for my fortune! Time you read for me.'

'You don't believe in the cards. You've always said so. Why should you have changed? You're trying to make a fool of me.'

'Chicken,' she taunted. 'Feeble. Scared you can't do it?'

'There's no point, April. Not if you don't believe.'

'Convince me.'

'Your disbelief will only colour the cards.'

'Prove yourself then. Prove your powers. Show me.'

'Show you what?'

'Show me what you can do.'

'Why should I bother?' I glanced up, caught April smiling round the room. She thought she'd won hands down.

'Okay,' I sighed. 'Sit down. You're on.'

The sixth year common room is not that large, and that day it was bouncing. Funny how a space can change. One moment it's a tangle of conversations, different worlds; the next it's unified. Consonant, even. As I gathered up the cards, eyes opened, ears became surreptitiously disentangled from iPods and mobile phones. Lunch was no longer an object. Sandwiches lay uneaten. Gossip failed. As I offered her the cards, you could have heard a pin drop. You could have heard it swishing through the air. Ellie and Elsa, April's joined-at-the-hip lifeskill partners slunk towards us. On my side, Jen and Bran stood by the radiator, as if covering my back.

I handed the pack to April. She received it uncertainly.

'Box it,' I nodded.

'What d'you mean? You've got the box.'

I raised one eyebrow this time. My right eyebrow. The only one I can raise independently, not having done the hours of eyebrow training all incipient film stars and right-minded babes put in these days.

'Shuffle the cards.'

This time April knew what I meant. She wasn't very good, kept dropping cards and having to stretch for them and slide them back into the disorganised pack.

'Okay,' I said eventually, 'now count out twenty-six. Good.' I watched her manicured hands dance above the table. I watched the weather too. It had started to rain. Heavy raindrops. Thunder-like.

'Now what?' April narrowed her eyes.

'Give what's left to me. You've shuffled the cards, halved the pack. You agree?'

She nodded.

'And I haven't touched them, not till now?'

Again she nodded. I swept the counted-out cards to the bottom of the pack.

'Right, let me see …' I laid the top three cards before her: Jack of Hearts, Ace of Diamonds and Seven of Spades. 'We want these to add up to ten,' I told her. 'Face cards count ten, Aces one. So …'

Leaving the Jack alone, I added nine cards to the Diamond, and spread a further three below the Spade, musing out loud the distribution of upturned rows.

'Interesting, April … what have we got here? More black than red. A jack. An ace.' I handed her the pack, what was left of it. 'I'd like you to count cards again. Count seventeen. The next card will be the Ace of Spades. That's my prediction.'

April, frowning, did as she was told. Ellie and Elsa helped, counting out the cards out loud. 'Sixteen … Seventeen …'

She turned the next card up.

'Ace of Spades!' This triumphant chorus from Jen and Bran. No surprise. They'd seen me in action before.

April was furious. 'You counted them!'

'How could I have done that?'

'I laid half of the pack face-up! You were watching, counting.'

'Was I, Ellie, Elsa? Was I watching?'

'No,' Ellie sounded confused. 'No, she was gazing round the room. She wasn't watching, April.'

Jen and Bran grinned. They had seen this reaction too.

'Fluke. I bet you couldn't do it again.'

'April,' I nodded to the clock. 'It's nearly five to two. I can do this again, or I could read your future. Once the bell goes you've lost your chance.'

She smiled, thinly. 'Do it again – and this time *with your back turned.*'

Jen and Bran looked worried now. This was something new. They knew how the trick worked. I'd shown them way back. The proof of good friends is their silence. When it matters.

'Will you or won't you?' April's voice would have frozen a sandy shore.

Jen and Bran looked at the clock and then their watches.

'April, that clock is slow,' Jen muttered. 'And it's physics next. Anderson's never chuffed if we're late.'

'As if,' said Bran, nonchalant, 'a little quantum rearrangement couldn't sort that out.'

April smelled victory.

'Will you or won't you?'

I looked at her directly. Didn't flinch. 'One or the other, April. If I do this, there won't be time to read your cards.'

'I'll bear that misfortune somehow.' She settled herself. 'Right. Shall we begin?'

She shuffled the cards, still awkward. This time she didn't drop them.

'No,' she ordered. 'Don't close your eyes. Turn your back.'

I swivelled in my chair. Jen and Bran seemed pale. I took care not to catch their eyes, staring up at the window, open this rainy summer's day, reflecting palely the light and movement in the room.

'Twenty-five, twenty-six. You can turn back *now*,' April said, exultant, sure she'd be the winner of this round. 'Go on. Lay them out.'

'You remember the rule? The rule of ten?' I kept my voice deliberate, soft and low.

The cards that turned up this time were the Jack of Diamonds, Three of Hearts and Ten of Clubs.

'Mmm ...' I laid a further seven cards below the three, every one a Spade. 'Ah, black predominance. I predict –' I looked at the clock; two minutes to the bell. 'I predict the card ... before the twenty-fourth will be the ... Ace of Spades.'

'Hah! Rubbish!' April laughed out loud. She took her time counting. Ellie and Elsa didn't help.

Jen and Bran stood frozen, scarcely breathing.

I could feel the room – and everyone inside it – focusing, condensing on that one point, the cards in April's hands, the cards as she laid them down.

'Twenty-one ...'

April was grinning less. She'd begun to wonder why the Ace had not yet shown.

'Twenty-two ...'

A Spade. The seven, not the ace. The silence in the room was now so thick it brushed against us, smooth as velvet.

'Twenty-three.'

She hesitated, reaching for the card – a slip of churned-up wood, drenched and pressed, steamed and printed, laminated, worn and creased by serial use, all-too-frequent passage through diverse hands sweat-drenched or cool – molecules jumping, jostling – electrons dipping freely from orbit to wild orbit.

April took a deep breath. 'Twenty-three.' She placed the card face down on the desk. 'Turn it over,' she demanded.

'No.' I shook my head. 'You'll say I changed it. Cheated.'

April's fingers hovered. Her eyes slid to the clock. Seven seconds to the bell.

'Hurry up!' Ellie urged.

And Jen and Bran, all of us in that room, held our breath and stared. Stared at April's fingers, slim and long. Piano fingers. (She did play the piano, really well.) Those fingers floated barely a centimetre from the card.

And still she did not pick it up.

She could not. I had never seen her so uncertain. I don't think any of us had. April looked grim as death. As white. Her hands shook. Sweat rippled her brow, crimping her black hair.

Elsa cracked.

'Come on!' She pushed her friend aside. 'I'll do it if you can't!'

She snatched at the card just as the bell erupted.

One reality ending. Another stuttering to begin.

The room lost focus.

'Elsa, for god's sake, show us the card!' Jen brought us back to order.

Elsa did not obey. She did not seem able to.

Her face was a picture. I can still see her standing there, the undisclosed card in her hand; light danced around, sketching that profile feminine and young, fingered the twist of curls swinging from her crown. The table in the foreground ached with cards; we did too, all of us, even

April, staring, staring.

Our Physics teacher told us once about this thought experiment concerning a cat. A cat in a lead box. A cat that might be dead or alive. Or both. Schrödinger's Cat. Schrödinger's experiment. One half of the box is radioactive. You don't know till you open it which half the cat is in, whether it's alive or has died of radiation. And while you don't know, the cat is both alive *and* dead – at least according to the Schrödinger's equations. Once you've opened the box you've gone beyond the possible, collapsing the vibrant array of probabilities.

Elsa had just done that.

Opened the box.

Lifted the card.

And she stood there, just like the girl in the photograph I saw today. She stood there presaging the narrative. Defying time until the second bell.

I'll leave you with that image, more honest than the one I glimpsed today in newsprint black and white.

But reflect on this.

Reflect.

Perhaps Schrödinger played cards? Perhaps he read them too?

For everybody – even the most rational – needs a bit of magic in their day. While Newton called this gravity, Einstein and Feynman knew the universe expands so fast not even shifting particles can fill the void.

And when you stop to look at it, the universe amazes. All that probability not focused here on earth, but catapulting three-dimensionally through time and space. Hope, brightening all it touches.

My mother was strong on hope.

As am I.

I have always had good reason to be.

Morag Henderson

Jenny of the Pockets

It was a hot day in Inverness. The sun drenched the city centre in light, saturating the buildings until they emitted a warm, weak glow of their own. The summer was reaching breaking point.

On the High Street, just up from the river, two young men stood at the edge of the pedestrianised section of road, each with a fiddle in a case tucked under his arm. The High Street used to be the centre of town before most of the shops moved out to the nearby retail park. The young men were standing across the road from the Town House, next to McDonalds. Street furniture littered the pedestrian walkway – benches and spindly water-parched bushes, council-watered flower-pots and faux-Victorian street signs – while a few Inverneesians weaved slowly around the obstacle course to peer in the windows at hot shop assistants. But most people did their shopping elsewhere these days, and used the town centre as a meeting-place. Knots of teenagers stood about, filling the street with yellow summer dresses, long legs and laughter. Parents took struggling babies out in pushchairs and sunhats, and tourists stared at everyone as if Inverness was a display in a theme park.

The two young men with the fiddles looked at the piper standing opposite McDonalds. His piping almost drowned out the sound of the guitarist in the close mid-way down the High Street, while around the corner in Inglis Street, at the other end of the pedestrianised section, a tiny girl in full Highland regalia enthralled the tourists by playing a clarsach almost as big as herself. There was no room in this part of town for any more buskers. The piper had told the two young men as much when he had stopped for a break, quickly and with a practiced hand counting out the coins from the open music case that lay at his feet, and sorting out the larger denominations to put in a safer place. 'Where are you from?' he had asked them, and when the lads had admitted to being from Cape Breton, he had broken into a smile. 'Everyone knows the best fiddlers come from Cape Breton. But listen, mate, I'm here all year round, you know. There's not much money in winter, and I have to make up for it in summer. I need the money to go to the RSAMD in

Glasgow for their new Celtic music course, like … you could try round the corner, see if Judith's packed up her clarsach for the afternoon yet.' He shouldered his pipes and stepped back to his position at the wall, posing for photos with happy tourists who shook his hand and left him another few coins. 'Good luck, MacMasters!' he called over to Calum and Finlay, whose Scottish names marked them out as sons of ancestry-obsessed New Worlders.

Inverness used to be a town. It used to be a place where you could walk down the High Street and it would take all day because you had to stop and talk to everyone that you knew. It was made a city by the Queen for the millennium, and the small town grown large had not yet adjusted to its new status. It was as if there were two Invernesses side by side, uneasily co-existing in the thundery air. One was full of new people: incomers who walked through anonymous city streets where they knew no-one and shopped in chain stores; and one full of people who stopped to talk, who knew each others' parents and remembered what had happened to them all together when they were sixteen and first saw summers like this.

Old men who had forgotten the conventions they grew up in, but who had not adjusted to living in a city, lurked in shadows and old Inverneesian pub corners. But old women who forget conventions were suddenly out in the summer air, walking along the streets of the town every day where previously they would have been living an indoor life. Jenny, for example: she kept herself clean and neat, she caused no trouble – but she was always around, always walking through town. That was how you knew she was mad. That, and the pockets: she was smartly dressed, with little black-heeled shoes with a shiny gold buckle on the front, but all over her clothes she had sewn extra pockets. She was known in Inverness as Jenny of the Pockets.

Jenny of the Pockets saw the two young men from Cape Breton with their fiddles on her way back from lunch at the bookshop. The second-hand bookshop was one of her favourite places in town. She liked the real wood fire in the middle of the shop, and sometimes stood looking into the flames in winter, watching the orange and the smoke twisting together up the chimney. She liked the Scottish section of books, where she pulled out old volumes on the history of Inverness and took them upstairs with her to the café. 'When I was young,' she told the waitress, 'they used to tell greedy people like myself that we would come to a bad end. That when we walked into church, God would see us and our wickedness and turn us into stone, and then we would shatter into smoke and dust.' The waitress was an older woman with a family, who only worked at weekends.

'Oh, I'm sure you're not wicked now,' she would reply, clearing away Jenny of the Pockets' plate with the left-over crumbs of chocolate cake.

'It seems I'm not,' said Jenny, with her brilliant smile, 'because here I am quite happy in church with a cup of tea. Did you know this used to be the old Gaelic church, this building?' The waitress nodded because of course she knew that, but she had to work: there were other people's plates to be cleared away and other customers to be served.

'You take care of yourself now, Jenny,' she said as she bustled away. Jenny of the Pockets dabbed genteelly at her mouth with her napkin and left the waitress a good tip.

Calum and Finlay were from the northernmost part of Cape Breton. When the first Scottish emigrants arrived there, they had thought that it looked like their home country, which many of them had not wanted to leave. The winters were harsher though, but those of the Scots who survived kept alive their musical traditions. It was true what the piper said, that the best fiddlers came from Cape Breton. Calum and Finlay had grown up in a place more Scottish than Scotland, and they looked in Inverness as if they could almost be locals – if it wasn't for something indefinably different about them. But they weren't talking about that when they walked down the street and Jenny followed them. They were talking about money, and whether or not they could find jobs. Because they were Canadian, their accents were naturally slightly louder than the Inverneesians around them, and Jenny found it quite easy to hear what they were saying. Jenny thought that the difference between the Nova Scotians and the Inverneesians was perhaps that the Canadians looked somehow cleaner. But she liked their matching red hair, which gleamed in the sunlight.

Calum and Finlay were nice boys; they were polite and they held the door open for Jenny as they walked into a pub – one they had chosen because of its name: it was called after the battle that had been fought near to Inverness. 'After you, ma'am,' they said.

'Thank you,' croaked Jenny, in her little-old-lady voice. The boys thought she sounded like a heavy smoker. She sailed through the bar and into the back where the toilets were.

'What can I get for you?' asked a cheerful and distinctively Australian voice. The barmaid was pretty and dark; sturdy. The room was dark too, and stuffy. Summer had reached inside the pub, but it had not lightened the place – just kept it preserved, in a holding pattern until night-time. Or until autumn, when it would be cool enough again to want to spend time indoors. 'Do you serve food here?' asked Calum, who was the older of the two boys. They were so close, they were like brothers. 'Yeah,' said the barmaid, and showed them the list on the wall: baguettes and ciabattas and other Italian-sounding foodstuffs. Her boss, a large man who looked like his grandfather, stood at the other side of the bar. He knew what was going on, though he didn't watch his employee openly. Calum and Finlay studied the list and chose; and then they chatted with the Australian about her time in Inverness, about whether it was hard or not to get a job, about whether or not she liked it here. She liked the town, mostly for the friendly people she had met, and she was happy to elaborate on the night-life, which was the thing she loved most. Finlay raised polite eyebrows when she asked if they were American, but since she didn't seem to know where Cape Breton was, he didn't elaborate. In that way he was quite Inverneesian. He was quieter than Calum, but just because they were both quiet didn't mean they were both timid; it just made them a little harder to get to know.

'An orange juice, please,' asked the Jenny of the Pockets in her polite but harsh voice. The barman knew Jenny, had seen her around town for years. She was the one who always told him he looked like his grandfather – which he liked, because his grandfather had been a good man. The barman thought Jenny was a tinker, one of the old families, and he called her Mrs MacPhee.

'There's no need for you to buy anything if you just wanted to use the loos,' he told her.

'No,' said Mrs MacPhee. She took the tall glass and sipped politely at the juice.

'Where have you been out to?' The Australian girl continued her conversation. 'I mean, other bars? This place has a fair amount, you know, but there's some crazy parties if you know where to go.' She leaned in conspiratorially. 'Have you been up Tomnahurich hill? Or out to Clava cairns? Magic mushrooms, you know, that's where to get them.'

Calum and Finlay, sophisticates as most Cape Bretoners are, nodded. Their attention was drawn by Jenny of the Pockets and the barman.

'Why do you think she has all those pockets?' whispered the Australian barmaid. Mrs MacPhee, quicker of hearing than expected, stood at the other side of the bar and looked at Calum and Finlay.

'To keep my money in,' she said, and flashed a coin as bright as her sudden smile.

The barman had found that his Australian barmaid did a little less work than he would have liked. He looked disapprovingly at her as Jenny left, her orange juice unfinished, and the barmaid continued to chat with the two lads from Canada. 'There's work for you to do through the back,' he said heavily. 'Unpacking.' His speech fell into the light, modern conversation about parties and drugs and money as if the words were heavy old-fashioned boxes. 'And you lads.' He finished each phrase with a pause like a full stop. 'You can take those sandwiches away with you if you like. Nice day like this, young people like yourselves should be outside.'

Calum and Finlay ate the remainder of their baguettes on a bench nearby, outside a car park, watching the seagulls swoop down low over Farraline Park bus station. Jenny knew the town better, and she was sitting at a bench up by the castle. She liked to look at the statue of Flora MacDonald, who was always looking down the drive to see what was coming next. If she turned one way, Jenny could see down to the river and the houses and the cathedral on the other side of the water, and if she turned the other she could see the old buildings on Castle Street. She smiled brightly to herself, appreciating her home, and tourists moved to get away from her and make sure she wasn't in their pictures of poor Flora.

Other people had seen Calum and Finlay too, and other people than Jenny knew that they were looking for work. As the evening drew on, Judith packed up her clarsach and went home, and the two boys played for a while in her old busking site till one of the workers from one of the cafés asked them to move on. They said that the pavement belonged to the café; that they had their tables out there; that Calum and Finlay were disturbing the customers. But the Cape Bretoners had made some money by then, and they mollified the barista by buying some juice. They drank it at one of her silver outdoor tables, still warm from the sun's rays, as they counted the change that passers-by had thrown in the hats at their feet. A man was watching them from the other table. He was wearing a tweed jacket, despite the heat, and he had thick black hair and sparkling blue eyes. He looked exactly as Calum and Finlay thought that Scottish people should look, and they were happy to talk to him when he came over to their table. He asked them where they had got their fiddles from, and how it was that two boys not from Inverness could know some of the old Gaelic tunes from so long ago.

As evening drew in and the cafés closed, and people began to go home for something more substantial to eat, the town centre – or the little pedestrianised bit that Calum and Finlay now felt they knew so well – started to get quieter and quieter. The night was heavy and sticky and full of whispered promise. Jenny sat with her eyes closed up by the Town House, her hands occasionally reaching out to stroke the warm stone next to her as it cooled down. 'You know,' said the man with the tweed jacket and the thick dark hair, 'there might be somewhere you can make a bit of money tonight.' He paused expectantly. 'If you're looking for money, that is.' Calum looked at Finlay.

'We're looking for work, yes,' he said. The tweed man's blue eyes sparkled with enthusiasm. He knew so much and talked so passionately about music that the Nova Scotians were happy to trust him: the archetypical Scot.

'It's a party that's happening, over the hill. They could be looking for some musicians, could be happy to give you a wee something for your trouble.'

'Over the hill, eh?' said Calum, smiling. 'We heard today from a barmaid that that's where all the best parties were. She was talking about magic mushrooms and everything.'

'Magic mushrooms, right enough,' chuckled the old man, as though he found young people terribly funny.

Jenny of the Pockets watched as the two boys followed the tweed man across the bridge over the river.

Tomnahurich wasn't far for two young, fit lads to walk. It was the old town cemetery, and in the twilight – night took a long time to fall this far north in midsummer – Calum and Finlay felt it was a calm and beautiful place. Inverness lay below them, shimmering in the heat. It was a little bit of a longer walk for an older woman, and Jenny of the

Pockets caught up with them only at the last minute. The tweed man was holding the trees and grass back like a curtain and ushering the two musicians into the hill. Inside, Jenny caught a familiar glimpse of fairy dancers at a ceilidh that never stopped. The two boys from Cape Breton who were so anxious to discover Scotland didn't even look back as they stepped into Tomnahurich.

Jenny of the Pockets sat down, panting a little from the exertion of her walk out of town. She leaned against one of the gravestones. She patted the headstone, and read the name. 'Well, Thomas Mackenzie, merchant of the town, you found your Janet, and you had your children as well. I'm sure you provided well for them, or they wouldn't have left you this fine gravestone. It's always best to work for love, not money. I know that now; that's my advice as an old woman.' She looked out over Inverness, which was coming to life again now that people had rested and eaten their evening meal. 'Best to sing for love not money,' she croaked, and she reached into one of her many pockets and brought out a piece of fairy gold. It glinted as the sun set and the air finally cooled down, like a fever breaking.

Kevin MacNeil

Prayer, with Deaths

Lord,

Thou great big lump of omiscience, know this. It is Saturday night and the rain is flinging itself around in vast angry sheets. I feel that we've always had a tacit deal; you don't ask much of me, I don't ask much of you. A lifetime of worship in return for ... well, listen.

I am thinking of Mildred Veronitude, who died in a mild car crash because she was chewing bubble gum at the time of impact. I recall Farquhar MacDevitt, who invented a single brilliant joke and died of apoplexy when he saw it repeated verbatim in a Hollywood B-movie.

I remember Joey Skwegs, who decapitated himself blowing kisses to his girlfriend from the departing train; she'd been warning, not waving. I need hardly mention Baldy Goldsmith who, on his one hundredth birthday, died of an eighteen year-old blonde, a ten year-old malt and an eighty year-old itch.

Murray the Roundabout, you'll not forget, went mad and crushed his skull trying to turn his living room wall into a hat, having watched the film *Groundhog Day* once every day since it came out.

You know all about that weathergirl, Jemima C. Bloom, who suffocated on her own underwear in a Kansas tornado.

In your scheme of things, such deaths help sustain us. I like you best when you're being entertaining.

So, Lord, I ask of you only this. Let me die in absurdity. Let me have a witty gravestone. Let me die with a shocked smile on my face.

Then I shall forgive you.

Cheers and Amen,

You-Know-Who.

Donald S. Murray

Sandreel

Little Jenny digs with her red spade and bucket, scooping swirls of
sand into the air. Some rains on her head and clothes: the pink dress
her mother forced her to wear that morning. Soon, the white shower
that she swishes into existence covers her hair and skin, crusting her
mouth and eyelids – every inch of her. Finally aware of what's going
on, her mother jabs a finger in the girl's direction.

'No! No!' she shouts. 'Naughty! Naughty! You're making a mess of
your nice clean clothes!'

She jerks Jenny to her feet, gathering her up as she yells.

'You've got sand everywhere! Sand everywhere!' she cries.

Jenny begins to cry, spade dropping from her fingers as her mother
shouts.

'You've not to make a mess of your pretty clothes! You've not to!'

A short distance away, the sandreel begins moving, whirled into
existence by wind rolling across the foreshore. Part dervish and part
demon, he billows and rises from the beach, at first only a small
disturbance on the shoreline. Angry at being shaken from sleep by the
way that humans mistreat their children, he tears himself loose from his
moorings. A gyre of dust and sand-specks, he threatens the full force
of his anger – becoming once again the destroyer he has been so often
in the island's history. In 1748 when he tore away much of its edge. In
1823 when a village was destroyed, its homes and acres smothered and
stilled.

After a moment or two it dies down, only to rise again a few years
later in Jenny's life. Once more he is awakened by the way she has been
treated. This time she is lying on her back upon a dune guarding the rear
of the beach, a giant bank of sand some twelve or more feet high. On
its crest are waves of marram grass set in place to prevent the sandreel
from performing his ritual dance, stripping away the surface of the
land, allowing the ocean to run amok in places where houses have long
stood.

And Jenny is creating sand angels, stretching out and swirling arms and legs as if she is swimming in the ocean not far away. Her limbs move together in perfect symmetry. Absolute congruence. She looks at the tracks and traces left behind in the sand. It is as if feathers etch out her movements, trailing evidence of the way she has fashioned half-circles on the ground. She masters heaven. Defies gravity. Swirls and swoops to leave behind both earth and humanity behind for a time.

'What the hell are you up to?'

It is her father's voice, complete with an edge of drunkenness that frightens the twelve year-old. She has heard it too many times before.

'You've made a bloody mess of yourself again, haven't you? Sand in your clothes. Sand in your hair. God. We can't take you anywhere, can we?'

The sandreel begins again, swishing across the beach in anger, gathering dust and sticks and plastic as he whips across the shore ...

Some people, of course, do not call him the sandreel.

For them, he might be a sandstorm. The whisper of his arrival – a gentle swirl around a man's legs, the sigh of a breeze – creates visions of the bleak and empty spaces of the Sahara. They see Bedouin and camel, the men of the French Foreign Legion standing with weapons primed on the ramparts of a desert fort. Or it might be those from Britain's imperial past. Gordon of Khartoum. Lawrence of Arabia. Scimitar raised against rifle. Crescent against cross.

Or he could be a vision from another type of reel. The one that contained images of Oz and Kansas; Dorothy's home blown away by the force of a tornado able to swish and unsettle any young girl's head. Or the childhood story of the Sandman. How he sprinkled dust into the eyes of children, ushering into their nights either the pleasant hush of dreams or the howls of nightmares, darkening their sight for hours on end.

But to the people of this island, he is the sandreel. Or *danns a'gainmheach*, to those familiar with another tongue. They know him from the way he has jigged and swayed upon the foreshore, gathering everything he has come across into the rhythm and pattern of his dance. A vortex of dust and sand: even the waves become his partner. His beat and energy unrelenting, he links arms with winds and storms. Stones and boulders swirl in his grip, clutched for a short time before they are let loose and smashed against fence and crofthouse wall. An iron buoy is hurled inside the garden of someone's house.

It was the war that last let him loose. He started timidly enough – a pale imitation, perhaps, of the stunted figure of General Franco clacking castanets and performing a flamenco dance on the land's edge. Then he took on the form of Mussolini. A glower. Theatrical show of pomp. Pounding of chest and jerk of arm. The awareness as he swirled round that his every movement and threat of force was chiefly for display.

He grew angrier later. There was his impersonation of Hitler. The stamping of heels. That outstretched hand. It scythed seaweed, bringing down a hail of shingle on land near shore. It threatened blitzberg on the houses a half-mile or so from the beach, laying waste to their crops, burning acres with the scorch of sand.

A couple of incidents made him act this way.

A supply boat near the island sunk by a submarine's torpedoes.

A warship to the west strafed by planes.

Old Uilleam, too, weaving across the shore with the clink of glass accompanying every step. He had obtained the bottles from a shipwreck that had taken place a few miles to the south. Containing a cargo of whisky, he had been one of many who went out to plunder its hoard.

His wife Marsali was following him, her voice jagged as a bottle smashed on rock.

'Uilleam … Leave the drink. You've got a family to feed and care for at home. There's work to do. Leave the drink alone.'

'Och, woman,' he mumbled, shaking his head. 'It's only a bit of fun. All the lads are doing it.'

'But Seamus and Anna are hungry, *a' ghraidh*. There's no food in the house for them. Nothing at all.'

'Stop your blether. You're exaggerating. Leave me alone.'

'Listen to me …'

The sandreel did. He swept up from his resting place on the beach and swirled around the two of them. Uilleam felt the stab of sand on his face, scalding his cheek.

'God …'

The smack of grains blinded him. They burnt his skin, drawing his mouth tight. Even the back of the hand he pulled up to protect his face grew red and raw.

Yet his only response was to raise his bottle, swallowing yet another mouthful of whisky.

It was a little time after that the sandreel really let loose.

He heard tears and yells from inside the walls of Uilleam's house.

'There's peats to be cut.'

'We need to plant potatoes if we're to eat next winter.'

'What about the cattle?'

Ice edged the sandreel as he danced that month. Snow whirled among sand-grains, every gust bristling like sharp tips of flint. He bruised and bled men, as if he rose out of the Arctic with the rampaging force of Stalin and his Red Army. With the tide and storm as allies, he stamped earth with the fervour of a Cossack dance, destroying the few acres where even William managed to plant crops most years.

Finally, he reeled around their house, lashing its wooden door with his fists, pounding windows. Sparks of sand were fanned into greater fury, becoming flames. And, too, there appeared to be the turmoil and confusion of smoke, as the sandreel gathered all within its fury, darkening sky.

And in the morning, Uilleam and his family dug their way out the door of their home, studying the desolation covering all that had once been their land.

'We can't stay here any more, Uilleam,' Marsali said. 'There's no life left in this soil.'

He's moving once again – that sandreel urged on by storm and sea, two other forces that have had enough of man's stewardship of the earth. He's given power, too, by man's mishaps and mistakes. The way he bridged a narrow ford of waters by building a causeway in the wrong place. Or how he tried to shore up a promontory that should have been the ocean's property years ago. There is also the way the sea-levels are rising, the depth of waters increased by melting snow far north and south. All of this has given the sandreel a greater sense of his own power and fury.

He's heard, too, of what has happened in other lands. The place where the Tigris and Euphrates meet. The old desert kingdoms of Babylon and Nineveh. And he mourns all that has happened there. The spilling of salt tears and blood. Oil staining its surface. In response, he tries on the shifting shapes of politicians, swift and glib in their lies and evasions. A never-ending swirl. He becomes, too, an Army General, pounding up and down in self-importance. A bomber plane flying, leaving small explosions in its wake.

Yet mostly, he's angered by what's going on in Jenny's house. The petty cruelties. The small acts of drunkenness.

'Is Dad ever going to be sober?' he hears her yell. 'Mam! Why don't you stand up to him? Stop drinking yourself. Get out of all this.'

He groans and sighs, gathering his strength. Someday, when she leaves there, he's going to huff and puff and blow that stone house down …

David Knowles

Shin

Loch Shin's heart twice broken.
First by draining east
to firths and mud flats
away from the Highland cousins
of her mountain childhood,
west-coast brigands
whooping and hollering down to the Minches.

Then by the hydro-dam
concrete hysterectomy
leaving her headwaters silent
as a rung bell, hollow
longing for salmon.

Bitterly she persists
too long in a mourning of peat-black.
Hair dyed sitka green,
acidic rinses stunt the growth
of dark-bellied brown trout.
Foster children, galling the memory
of fresh-run silver.

David Knowles

The Language of Trains

The worst sounds are probably the trains that are not really trains. On balance, they are marginally more disturbing than the mysterious industrial process that continues off and on through the night. Then there are the drunks that wander by in the street below my third floor window. We would not call it a third floor at home. We would say it was an attic. But Mrs Myers calls it the third floor, and I must learn to articulate with all the subtleties of her native tongue. The drunks caused me great disquiet when I first arrived. One can never actually apprehend what drunks in the street are saying, no matter how vociferous they become. Not even at home in Poland. The wind and the street-lights shred their communiqués into syllables, as if disposing of top-secret documentation. But at home the syllables at least are familiar, not jagged and alien.

You will have noticed it by now. I am speaking as if I have a dictionary open at my bedside. Not literally, of course – it is dark in this malodorous room where I try to sleep. If I left the light on, Mrs Myers would speak to me about it again. Also, the filament of the naked bulb would burn into my eyes. I thought at first that it was just the way the pillow angled my head. It seemed impossible not to look directly at the light. On reflection, I realised that the shape of the bulb is not quite like any bulb we have at home. The outline is broadly similar but the proportions are slightly different. It traps the eye like a tongue returning to a broken tooth. So, no, I don't really have a dictionary at the bedside. But at night, when I cannot sleep, I allow myself the luxury of thinking in Polish. Not that I spoke in this florid, vocabulary-laden way at home. There I was a concise and straightforward speaker. It is just a luxury. Like a warm bath which is not available here because Mrs Myers says that showers are more hygienic. Words are a luxury. All the nuanced, obscure, overburdened or archaic Polish words that I can remember the meaning of, and some I only thought I knew the meaning of as I skimmed over them in a column of newsprint.

It is a weakness, I know. To allow myself to think in Polish is foolish. I will need accomplished English to market my idea and not have it taken away from me. In the first months I was resolute. When the

53

mysterious industrial process kept me awake I would discourse with myself in English about its possible meaning. It is a combination of sounds which could not be heard in Poland. We have many industrial sounds but not like these. Even after long hours of sleepless analysis I can form no satisfactory hypothesis as to the origin. The trains are another *kettle of fish*. I say this in English. Do you see! Say it quickly a few times – *kettle of fish, kettle of fish*. That is a British train. Unlike the mysterious industrial process I could surely recognise this as a train. But not a Polish train. They do not say these words. It must be the length of the track sections or the construction of the bogeys. I do not know. I did not work on the railways. I do know that even the trains here speak a language I struggle with. Yet in the beginning I could be strong and not relapse into Polish. In the beginning I could open the little drawer by the side of the bed and look at my idea. It was a great comfort and source of strength. Just to take it out and look at it for a moment. That is impossible now. The idea is still kept in the drawer just a few inches from my head. But I cannot allow myself to take it out.

No, I cannot tell you the precise nature of my idea. For two reasons. Firstly, if I told you then you would go off and become a millionaire and leave me with nothing. *I have little joke with you, no? Or not, maybe?* Because it is such a good idea if I can just get it started. I can tell you only this much. Think of successful new commodities from the last few decades. Think of the ones which combine the pleasure of a hobby with the harmless vice of forming a collection and maybe the chance to show off to your friends. That makes a good idea. Now add the chance to turn your hobby into a business and you have a really great idea. I have such an idea and I have brought it here because here you have a real passion for hobbies. Also, and I do not mean to be rude, the credulity to believe you are all really going to make money out of my idea. You secretly believe that money really does *grow on trees*.

If confidentiality were all there was to it then you and I might have been able to come to some arrangement whereby I gave you a few more details. But then there is a second reason for my reticence – which requires me to be even more particular about the sharing of my idea. Because there is a problem. Not with the idea itself: I have absolute faith in it. Rather with the maintenance of the idea. I first noticed it about a month after I arrived.

I had secured employment of a sort at the *bookies* around the corner from my lodging. Mostly errands and clearing up. Remuneration in cash. It was not what I was used to but it kept *the wolves from the door.* We have a similar expression in Poland. *I make a joke to keep Mrs Myers from the door. Ha!* Nonetheless, I had hoped to meet people with an entrepreneurial bent, gambling men who might *'take a punt'* on a good idea.

At the betting shop I sometimes met a man called *Colonel George.* Colonels were important men in the old days in Poland. He wore a jacket and tie and called me *'old boy.'* The other punters *'tugged their forelocks'* when George came in and he made a little wave of the hand and said *'Good morning'* or most likely *'Good afternoon.'* I am cautious about strangers and checked with Andrea behind the counter. She is kind to me and sometimes makes me tea if it is quiet. *'Oh for sure, George is a real man of substance.'* She smiled. And she said that she was *'pretty sure'* what the substance was.

The next time I had an errand to run and Colonel George had placed his bet, I *'make my move.'* I supposed that he must be a busy man but he was kind enough to spare me some time. We went to the Dog and Duck. I bought him a *'pint of the best'* and a *'soda and whisky.'* It was business, and business has expenses. I would have to sell something else to Mrs Myers. Colonel George did not drink at work but since we were new business colleagues he said that it was *'quite in order.'* I had to tell him something of my idea. *Just enough to make his interest. I must make the idea in English and I feel I wrap a very soft thing in a rough sacking.* But it had to be done. He thought for a moment. He would *'get back to me soon'* and *'must dash, old boy.'*

That night the sound of foreign trains made me especially homesick. I put on the light and took the idea out of the drawer. It seemed to me that it looked slightly different, almost as if it had become a little bit transparent, the delicate cloth a little frayed around the edges. I keep a small collection of press cuttings with it to give credibility to my proposals. My eyes must have been tired because the print seemed to blur and swim. I put the idea back in the drawer and lay awake waiting for the mysterious industrial process. I would again try to imagine what it was, in English, and maybe this would allow me to fall asleep.

The next day at work I did not see Colonel George. I began to wonder if I had really explained my idea properly. I spent the afternoon re-phrasing my explanation in English. Careful to avoid giving the game away, I asked Andrea to explain the meaning of a few words I thought might be useful. The words seemed rough and lifeless but I had no choice but to wrap the idea in them. While I swept I practiced and revised my *sales pitch*.

After the afternoon of rehearsals there was no doubt. When I took the idea out of my coat pocket the colour of my hand faintly showed through as it rested on my palm. Some of the fine stitching at the edges had been torn and come away. I knew I had to do something quickly. I wrote beautiful Polish words on a sheet of paper and wrapped up the idea before putting it in the drawer. So now, when I cannot sleep, I allow myself to think in Polish. It is too risky to expose the idea, even for a moment of comfort in a sleepless night. There must be some corrosive element in the sound of the trains or the rough English words or perhaps in the mysterious industrial process itself. Colonel George will *'get back to me'* soon and I must be sure to keep the idea safe until then.

Peter Urpeth

The Clearing

Munzie Donald sat upright in his bed, content that everything was the same today as it had been yesterday. The daylight had the same hue of lichen, tinged with the dark green glow of the forest's dampness, and the wind still blew through the open slatted sides of the box in which he now lived and onto his naked face and arms.

On brighter mornings such as this, Munzie would open the hessian drape that hung across the doorway of the box – not a doorway but a crude hole – and he'd look out over the clearing toward the stand of Scots Pine that ringed the nearby lake. The redness of the gnarled bark on the uppermost reaches of the tree trunks caught the sun, and that sight, more than any other in the forest, calmed him and placated his anxieties.

For a moment, in that morning light – a moment lit by the quiet beauty of the forest – Munzie was free of the past. He could live as though he were innocent of life itself and, as if to embrace that feeling more fully, it was on these mornings that he would bathe in the weed-green water of the lake, feeling in its clammy coldness an echo of what remained to him of sensuality.

'Lake' was a word he would use to describe that stretch of water to himself, knowingly avoiding the fact that this 'lake' was no more nor less than a flooded swamp, and was no more than two feet deep at its deepest part. It was, in truth, a bog bunged with slurry; a safe hole that more often than not would freeze hard as slate in winter. When fully liquid, its water was languid, as though it had become solid in some other way than by freezing.

A mound of earth and stones ran around the lake's northern bank, its surface over-grown as though it were natural and certainly permanent. A man-made thing of some antiquity, he thought: a place of burial, sacrifice, religion in its own way and time.

Perhaps, thought Munzie, it was the blood of human sacrifice conducted on that bank that had over many years thickened the brackish water of the lake – water that was more broth than brine, except when his own urine thinned its margins in the early morning.

If the box, the lake and the clearing were a totality, an entire world no more than a few acres in absolute, then they were so because he'd deemed them to be a totality. His totality, his outer margins, staked out not as an act of possession but as an act of limitation: the imposition of boundaries, of lines, a methodology, even, that posited the knowable and displaced the infinite complexities of uncertainty.

The same physical, geographic act of limitation found its mirror in his own mind. The acquisition of the box represented the acquisition of a kind of mental boundary, and with that he could live. He cared very little for what had been before; memory was to be largely banished to the beyond; reality would consist of a few acres of the bearable both inside and outside his head, and that was all.

When recollection freed its hound into that space he'd snare it; exterminate the brute before its baying became incessant and the comfort of his vacant mind was invaded.

Then, with memory banished, the pain would stop and a calm acceptance would free him from the rigidity of his thoughts. When this happened he would walk to the mound at the very edge of the clearing and look out beyond the forest into another place. From on top of the mound he'd see the faint outline of hills and mountains away north, in the far distance.

Once, he stood and watched from that spot on a summer evening when the sun had gone down and the air had chilled, and he persuaded himself that he'd seen smoke curling above distant trees. The fire-smoke of some hermit, perhaps. The sight made him weep with longing and through his tears he'd called out, not *a* name, not *his own* name or the imagined name of the owner of that distant fire, but an awkward, almost barking grunt – the animality of which had shocked him into silence.

But today, like so many other days, Munzie clambered from the box. The cold night had set his bones as though the box were a mould for the renewal of disfigured humanity, and he stood awkwardly, cast in the statuesque forms of arthritis or rheumatism or other solid diseases of the loam. He could barely walk at first, and he stretched his body, hearing his bones and joints creak and crack like tree branches in a storm.

When straightened, he walked toward the lake and then he stripped naked, his flesh the colour of last year's reeds. A crow cawed as Munzie's toe broke the lake's watery mirror, and the heron that always stood on the far side of the lagoon loped away, its winging as rigid as Munzie's own movement – prehensile, prehistoric.

Munzie stood in the water, distracted by the ugly beauty of the bird. The heron's face was distorted: distorted, thought Munzie, by its anger: a rage that stalked it through all the millennia of its evolution until its face was so badly contorted it had become elongated at the mouth and nose; its skull scalpiform, ready to cut the air.

After placing a first toe in the lake, Munzie leaned into the water's dirt. The swamp was too shallow for diving, and too shallow even for swimming but he'd loll in its substance, its mix of damp and solids and things that somehow were in between those states – ambiguous matter, part plant, part sediment – hermaphroditic (as are all lakes) – amphibious, a mass of toe-caught annoyance that housed simple creatures that were themselves, in all probability, early in their evolutionary phases and, like Nature's babies, would suck at anything.

How long Munzie had lived in this place, he could not now be sure. He knew, though, that it had not always been *his* place, *his* home, and he'd inherited it from a pioneer of the forest who, Munzie postulated, had reclaimed that small patch of land beneath the box maybe thirty years before.

But there was no evidence of that time-span, nothing hard or fast to go on, no ruins or salvage, and Munzie was, of course, grateful – very grateful, even sentimental with gratitude for the home he now had. In evening light, he'd weep a flood of dry tears (maybe, in truth, more laughter than weeping) just thinking of the last time he saw that pioneering soul alive, sitting outside that same box by that same lake in that same clearing with those pines.

It was Adam that he saw: Adam without Eve. Innocent Adam, and innocent he remained even though Munzie had seen that self-same, spartan Adam masturbating by the lake until, with a single grunt that raised the heron from its stare, his white milk hung from his fingers and in the brackish water, and slowly sank to a place amongst the other spawn of that bog.

As he sat in the lake this morning, his legs submerged, his torso mud-caked and frozen, Munzie thought of the nights he hung around that man, keeping a distance so that he would not be seen. Watching from the clutter of branches mid-way up the beech tree by the back of the box until he could see that the man was inside, asleep.

How he had not been detected, he did not know. Stalking, hiding, the skillful pursuit of quarry: these were not Munzie's gifts in the wild. Had that man not wondered why the birds weren't singing? Had he not thought why the owl had gone from its perch? Did he not know that things were disturbed, not normal, not quiet in their ordinary way but quiet with suspense and apprehension?

On the night of the hand-over, the climb down the smooth trunk of the beech tree, soundless and blind in the darkness, was the hardest part for Munzie. Other than the stone he had secreted within hands'-reach of the drape when the man went to the lake that morning, surprise was his main weapon. And when he was safely on the ground that night, and at the side of the box, Munzie had not bothered drawing back the drape, he just reached inside and grabbed the man by whatever came first into his hands. It was the legs, the lower legs, the flares of his trousers (that gave such good grip) and Munzie hauled him out into the dark. The man yelled, for sure; a sickening yell quite suitable to the experience, almost tutored in all honesty, and Munzie pushed him back against the ground with his open hand on his chest and grabbed the secret stone. He brought it down in a single blow into the face of the man that stunned him into silence.

Then Munzie made another blow and another and then the man was limp apart from the sporadic and irrational jerking of his arms, and now Munzie could release the pressure on his chest and finish the job with both hands tight about the pungent, slippery weapon.

It was too dark that night to see the wounds in anything but outline, but touch and feel and smell told him that the wounds were serious and deep, bloody and free-flowing, not superficial in any way. And the smell of blood was coarse among the soft nose of rotten leaf mould they had disturbed in their struggle on the forest floor.

Munzie filled the man's vest (tucked into the belt of his trousers as it was) with stones and pulled him to the lakeside and kept on walking out into the deepest parts, dragging him beneath the surface. In the centre, or that place that Munzie felt to be the most central, he'd pushed him to the bottom and held his body down. Air bubbled out of the corpse for a while. Maybe it was the corpse venting or the air in his pockets escaping, and when the gurgling stopped Munzie lifted his hands and the body remained, weighted to the lakebed. He returned to the clearing and the box.

That first night in the box was one he often recalled. The interior was cramped, and the sleeper could only fit inside by curling his limbs and arching his back, but the box was unusually sturdy and would take the pressure of a man leaning on its side with ease. The hem of the drape was frayed and muddy, but still it kept out the wind and light sufficiently to give a man a good chance of sleep.

The morning after the killing, Munzie had walked to the lakeside. The water was flat calm and the body it held was not visible from the shore. Munzie relaxed, relieved that he'd done the job well and that all evidence of that cold, bloody killing was gone. He walked the lake edge and climbed a silver birch that overlooked the far side of the water. From height, his relief turned to horror. The submerged body was plain to see, or rather the face and head were distinguishable from the uniform greenness of the lakebed, and a rust stain of semi-set blood drifted slowly up from the body infusing the surrounding waters of the lake with a thin, sickly wash the colour of weak tea.

Anxiety rose rapidly in Munzie's mind. He should have turned him over, he knew, but in the hurry and excitement he'd forgotten the plan he'd made. It had all seemed too simple, too easy. He stared at the face, the sickly discharge, the bulging yellowed eyes, and he knew he'd have to recover the body. He knew as he sat in the birch that his haste had pinned him to the remains and a solution would have to be found. His anger rose. He leaned back on the branch and struck his forehead against the furrowed bark of the tree trunk. He struck it again and again, and the dull thud of his head echoed in the clearing and was soon joined by the rattle of a distant woodpecker eager for a mate or to secure its territory.

As he struck his head pain grew behind his eyes, and he struck his head again until all thought of the body was displaced from his thoughts. Dizzy with the blows, Munzie became unsteady in the branches and the lure of sleep came upon him. His head nodded forward and startled him awake. Slowly he leaned forward again and embraced the tree trunk with both arms and laid his head on its cold, indifferent bark and slept.

When he woke, evening light filled the clearing. The face was still visible in the lake and he knew that from then on, unless some other remedy could be found, he'd have to keep watch for visitors: keep them from the trees until the face had gone.

As he looked at him now, dead in the water, Munzie remembered how strange it was that of all the nights he had watched that man when he was alive, the night of his extinction was the one night on which that man had chosen to light a fire. Before turning in for the night the man had stamped it out, not half-heartedly but fiercely as though he hated its heat and its smoke only rose for a moment or two before fading to nothing.

Munzie would not have sat by another man's fire. Flame is like family, somehow part of a man, his property, and so Munzie was relieved that the man had put it out himself. By morning, the half-burnt logs and pile of ash were cold and Munzie kicked them away, scattering them to the rogue clumps of fern and bracken that grew beneath the trees and ringed the clearing.

In the weeks that followed the killing, Munzie had tried to find a solution to his visibility by filling the man's gaping mouth with stones hurled from the bank. Each shot would obscure the target by splashing and cascading rings toward the banks and disturbing deep-lying sediments. And then, after each throw, he would wait for the rings to calm and the mud to settle and then he'd throw again, hoping for a direct hit. But none came and over time the ritual of throwing acquired a metronomic certainty. He'd gather stones of a certain size and weight from the forest floor, and each in turn he'd throw toward the target. The gathering required him to search further and further out beyond his usual range, and the weight of the stones carried from a distance became an intolerable but necessary burden.

Then he'd wait for the rings to clear and the waiting was quite uniform and seemed to measure out time in regular intervals. The rings would die and the mud would settle. He'd throw again and wait for the rings to die and the mud to settle once more. And then one day he threw a stone and hit the sunken head and gashed it badly, turning the face slightly toward the bank and freeing something fluid from the skull or the skin, or from the gash of red and brown, or maybe an eye on its chord. The sight made Munzie retch out the mess he'd eaten that day, and thereafter the stone throwing stopped.

Once, he'd walked out into the lake and lay down beside the beaten man and stared upward through the thin film of water that covered their faces. For a moment he studied the scene above him, seeing the tree where he sat in the branches and the other familiar sights distorted by water. He was desperate to open his own mouth but not to talk; just to let the rank water fill his lungs, allowing him to drift, a slow drift, away from the clearing: a drift from life to death. But his will for life clamped his mouth shut and with a violent and revolting urge he stood bolt upright and coughed and spewed into the air.

But he did not want to think of those things now, today. His morning bathe over, he climbed from the water and walked back to the box. He dressed, putting back on the only clothing that he had. Now he would check his snares, and the thought of eating came strongly into his mind.

Munzie pushed through the waxy, bright green foliage of a rhododendron at the side of the clearing, and went to his snares at a place that had proven to be good for prey. One snare clutched the small red bundle of a squirrel. Its head had been distorted in its struggle for life, but he knew that its flesh would be good and sweet and would cook well and quickly.

Munzie returned to the box with his quarry and raked over the embers of a fire he had made a day or so before, kicking out the spent wood and charcoal. The clearing was silent. Then Munzie heard the thud of something heavy landing on the ground behind him. He turned instinctively to face the source of the noise, and saw the black outline of a large stone held tightly in a dirty hand closing quickly in on his face.

Peter Urpeth

Red Kites at Docherty

Above the fallen folly,
Amongst the ballet holds
Of the high pine stands,
Kite is silence
Gliding,
A russet hue
Skimmed on the
Flat blue
Of the winter day.

We counted them,
Three or five,
Talon-grappling
In a stall of wings,
Full of the fury-tangle
Of the prodigal.

Once exiled
From these
Haunted spaces,
They left the skies
Burnished with vastness,

Until the
Fancy ancestor
Returned,
With half
A memory
For the place.

Alison F. Napier

Flight

'So you're going.' It was a statement.
'Yes.'
'And are you coming back?'
'Yes.' It was a lie.

Behind you the brilliant white walls were decorated with abstract prints of blocks of colour and post-cards bought on far-away holidays – not with me – unframed and tacked on with drawing pins, and because it was February in England the central heating was stifling us at twenty-one degrees. You were perched on your large sagging dusty blue armchair, poised and waiting as I watched and faded you out. Faded you out, in your spacious and over-furnished high-ceilinged living room in a three-floored house in an elegant street in a terrible respectable and empty address.

You were talking. I can see the many rows of books around and behind you: millions of words about science and ecology, feminism and economics, politics of all shades and a sea of self-improvement manuals and it cannot – no, cannot be as simple as they claim. Beyond the ethnic lamps and incense burners I see a television and a video and an answering machine (*I detect a malfunction I detect a malfunction*, it drawls): communication for beginners.

You were apologising. I see a bottle of whisky and two glasses and two cold coffee mugs from earlier. The Hoover has not been put away, so somebody will trip over the flex. Boxes of personal possessions have – like my rage and other contents – yet to be unpacked, unleashed, unearthed; to be distributed in their appropriate final resting places.

You were still speaking and you handed me a drink; perhaps my fourth or fifth. But that liquid fire would not melt my chill, thaw my numb, warm my blood, for neither fire nor whisky can hope to plumb these depths and I fear I have been given up for dead. Hermetically sealed once more, and I fear I have been given up for dead.

Although, as ever, there is another way of looking at it. A powerful gentle passion previously unsuspected that woke sleeping senses and stroked and stoked with tender touch and tongue a woman I had never known and held me to you as I cried and wept into you at every point of contact. We became one, the poets would say, and ah my lover we became one and – yes. That is the other way of looking at it.

So they sealed us in, sealed us up, sealed us over, sealed us out. Your doors slide silently open as I approach them; I do not even have to touch. I cannot even choose; they open and I am consumed; I have to enter. The loiterers no doubt are crushed to death but I am in. The chaos I have left silent forever behind thick plate glass – buses and taxis spewing noiseless fumes, families and crowds mouthing voicelessly, all shimmering in the terrible heat of a transatlantic summer. But do not panic, for I am only in an airport. The future is so bright that I have to wear shades. The aging internationalists have touched up their tans and are absorbing the news-sheets and exclaiming at intervals How Dreadful How Shocking are the evils of our homelands; plastic Coca-Cola Land strikes again, but me: I am the United Nations in Bosnia-Herzegovina, I am Amnesty in Turkey, I am the doctor in the leukaemia ward, I am observing and reporting with little hope of change. I have entered an international airport; I am observing and reporting; I am walking on air.

In case I should have a bomb upon my person or in my baggage I have arrived four hours before departure. Four hours to kill, and so I will sample life in this brave new world. She hands me back my ticket. Have a good trip, now. I stare. Have a nice day. I stare. Already I have failed, for I do not speak the language and it is allegedly my own and I fear I have been given up for dead.

I left a woman warm and moist like compost, but nothing grew. I should have flourished but I was buried, smothered in soft brown earth, the peaty fusty smell of sweaty crevices and dusty toes. You do not know what you are asking as you bury me and I do not grow. Dead seeds and dried-out twigs will not take no matter how you water them and shower them with love. Give me up for dead, although I have not always been so brittle-dry and withered.

It's a hundred and ten outside, but in here it's cool and I'm looking for a coffee. I saw a Pizza Hut or a Burger King in – was it London or

Aberdeen? – and is this Houston or Miami or Minneapolis or somewhere else? – and irritation mounts and artificial air pricks my nostrils and my skin and my conscience.

On an island off my native Highland shore a woman from Tucson, Arizona gave me a massage and I fell in love with her for a day. We sat in a car outside a phone box and I muttered it, despairingly: I've decided I'm in love with you. Of course. So predictable. I was a vacuum into which anyone might fall. And the woman from Tucson, Arizona agreed with me and smiled kindly, if I recall correctly, and said yes. Just 'yes.' She was exploring Britain and her hands searched my back and stomach, chest and limbs, fingers forehead face, with the skill of a much-travelled woman. I tell what I know. Forgive me, Tucson, Arizona.

Down an escalator to pass the time and down another to a carpeted basement through which travels a satellite train, a tube, a two-sectioned unmanned space-age hi-tech transport bubble. Our Next Stop Is The Hotel Marriot Please Sit On The Seat Provided Our Next Stop Is but whose voice is this please? Have we met? And so I enter and sit and we purr through maroon deep-pile corridors deep beneath an airport, and it comes to a halt and we get off and our stainless steel bubble tube carries on and disappears.

Ever-hopeful, I go to the third floor Garden Café in a lift. I could have my Dunlop Green Flash gym shoes polished; I could buy a Stetson and a jar of chilli sauce in a basket full of straw. I could have my hair done or buy an outfit. Instead, I stride into the Garden Café with a confidence that I know does not convince. I don't know if I should find a seat or wait to be seated. I look for the garden and hover as waitresses and waiters hurry round me.

'Excuse me. Do I come to you or do you come to me?' I hear myself saying, unbelievably, to a woman in a dress with a name badge: Gina, who replies, 'I'm sorry?' 'Do I … I'd like a cup of coffee please, if …' But she is long gone. I am a vagrant who has failed to pass as an international traveller and it is little wonder. Jon the waiter, my saviour, now ushers me royally to a seat and the menu, huge and plastic like a windbreak, arrives with a flourish. There are so many decisions in this life – like pizzas and burgers with a wealth of toppings and chicken wings with a blue cheese dip and other flights of fancy – so I order nachos, knowing that it will not be too alien for this is an international airport, and lots of coffee. My watch says 10am. My body says 4am for I have crossed several time-zones and my stomach says nothing as a vast dish of tortilla chips, bean paste, guacamole, cream, salsa, all smothered with melted orange cheese with a green salad on the side and an unordered giant portion of chips arrives – this is such a gross and excessive country and I have been corrupted, so I tackle this feast bravely for time is on my side and I study it for evidence of life-giving properties but I am hungry and time is on my side.

There are air-hosts and air-hostesses; there is a pilot with his wife and child, the child exiled in a high-chair operations tower; at another table a young man in tight jeans and a mobile phone and a tee-shirt is talking to Grandpa from *The Waltons* with a long white beard, checked shirt, corduroy trousers and leather sandals. This is America, there is no garden, and now I remember where I am. I eat and watch, observing and reporting; I pay and leave. I investigate the toilet with its disposable paper toilet seat cover which claims to disappear as you flush, as may I, nervous behind a too-low stable door, and true: it does. I have to leave; I'm sorry but I have to leave. And the returning bubble tube is oblivious to my distress.

There was no garden.

My departure lounge was waiting and I wait and wait and wait. I read the New York Times; I detect a malfunction, I detect a malfunction. There is evidence to show that children as young as six months can comprehend mathematics, I read. If two items are added to two items and the result is five items then the child's gaze is perturbed. But my child, things never add up and we always put two and two together and make five. And the whole will always be bigger than the sum of its parts unless they are lying and, my child, they often lie. Believe me. They often lie.

'Passengers for flight CO 774 to Santiago with seats in rows twenty-four to forty-eight please prepare to board.'

As I have often lied.

Message in a Bottle

The twelve year-old Macallan had surpassed itself once more and now I was kneeling beside the loch – admittedly a little less than stone-cold sober – unscrewing the lid again and tipping what was left of it very slowly into the clear dark waters as they lapped against the pebbles on the shore.

Enough is enough. Klibreck loomed above me, its towering perfect reflection turning golden as the liquid gurgled out of the bottle and into the shallows. Such a waste, I thought. Such a bloody waste. I looked at the wooden rowing boat tethered to a rock on the small sandy beach, its paintwork flaking, the oarlocks rusty and empty, the oars tidily inside like wings folded ready for the next adventure, and I longed to stagger over and release it, to push it into the water and clamber in. But of course I didn't. And, of course, if I had done so I would have been stranded adrift in a land-locked loch as I tried to keep the oars in the locks, and falling backwards as the heavy wood failed to make contact with the water. I do not know how to row a boat. I imagine that I can, but like weightlessness, or walking on water, these skills are only available in dreams.

So I scrabbled amongst the gravel and sand and buried the empty whisky bottle. There was no message. The grassy bank up to the road was skitey and I wished I had worn the leather hiking boots that make me feel tough and rugged, make me feel that I am ready for anything, make me feel I can take on the world, vanquish foes, march forever onwards, live to fight another day. But of course I hadn't, so I reached the car in an ungainly scramble, with wet feet and scratches on my hands, whimpering to myself. 'Okay, okay. It's okay. Focus. Had a bit but not too much. Concentrate. Here we go, here we go, here we go.' I opened the car door, climbed in and felt for the ignition key in my pocket.

And it is not only in nightmares that the car keys are not where you know you put them. This new, modern and expensive mountaineering jacket has one hundred and forty-seven different pockets – or so it seems – and none of them contains my car keys as I frantically pat myself all over. Massage for the lonely. I test the two main pockets – the normal ones, I call them: the ones at each side. The ones you would put your gloves in if you had remembered to take them too; the ones you put your hands in when you need to hide, need to hold yourself together. They are not there. Nor are they in the map pocket, or the strange openings on the sleeves.

I have lost my car keys.

You would laugh at this now, if you were here. You would say, 'For God's sake, just look properly. You had them; you got here: ergo, they are here.'

Ergo? I had them; I lost them: ergo, I am stupid.

It is getting dark now; well after four o'clock, black clouds are filling the sky and Klibreck is a vast silkscreen silhouette. I look away, step carefully out of the car, walk round to the boot and find a torch and a blanket. I also find the other half-bottle that stays in the carrier bag with the screen wash and the sponge. I know how important it is to be one hundred percent prepared, and to cater for all eventualities. The quality has gone downhill but anything that is seventy percent proof is good enough for me. And I was so close to going home, so close. I really was.

So I slither back down the slope again and pick my way back across the shingle to the boat. It wobbles a bit as I clamber in, but stays stable once I have positioned myself on the seat, my feet avoiding the pool of rainwater on the bottom, the bottle resting against the gentle curve of the wood. Made to measure. The trick, it would appear, is never to leave dry land. Instead, to remain ashore, with feet firmly on the ground. How little I knew then, because before I knew what had happened I was all at sea.

But you were right, of course, and instead of a vague yet romantic tendency to periodic and poetic episodes, which was what I had hoped for in my anxious attempts to be interesting enough, I was instead just a bit too drunk a bit too often. I thought you wouldn't notice. I wanted to have ecstatic utopian visions and be an opium-eater. I wanted to be vivid and alive.

I wanted to be like you.

As well as the oystercatchers and the wind there is also now the sound of a car in the distance. Coming this way. Coming to find me. We have reports of an unidentified person trespassing in an estate rowing boat armed with a half-bottle of Teachers. Approach with care. We have reports of a life yet to be lived and of time disgracefully squandered. We have reports. Could do better. Oh come and find me and pin my arms to my sides in a fierce hug that takes my breath away and I will never put my hands in my pockets again. Be my mountain rescue and my emergency service.

I bound up the bank one final time, abandoning the whisky and the leaky boat, and take my seat in the passenger side of a warm and purring four-by-four. An orchestra drifts from the speakers and I smell new leather and stale smoke. Only the sweetness of *Old Holborn* can make me crave a cigarette and my fingers twitch with the need to be rolling tobacco. I am sure no-one will mind and I rummage in the glove compartment where I find the brown and orange plastic pouch complete with a packet of green papers. I am in heaven. And where are we off to, I ask? Where are we off to now? Home? Are you taking me home?

Home is red and silver and tinsel and a hat with a single tinkling bell sown into the tip. It is green shedding needles on a dusty carpet. Next year it must be artificial, we vowed. Well, we got that right. It is fragrant fruit and brandy that never catches alight, it is playing with fire. It is seas of shiny wrapping paper with the paddles hopelessly tangled in the string and weed-like ribbons that float just under the surface. And it is presents and pasts and tense futures. Home is where the heart has lost its nerve; home is missing in action.

My head has twelve drummers drumming in it and five gold rings tighten around my heart. The one on my finger has long gone. The elegant Jeep has also vanished and I am still huddled in my little rowing boat on the shore. I made it up. My half-bottle is still hugging the contours of the bows of my life raft and I reach for it with a shaking chilly gloveless hand. The water of life revives me and sets me on fire and I start to compose my festive message in my percussion-battered head. Here it is. Here it is now.

There is a biro in the map pocket; the blue plastic bit on the end has come off and the ink section is slipping in and out of the clear casing. So I throw the clear plastic bit onto the floor and just use the skinny ink bit, which is very awkward and keeps slipping through my fingers. I am writing on the back of a supermarket receipt. I read the story of my messages first: mince and potatoes and carrots and turnip, one-litre bottle of whisky, three-litre box of French red wine, and twenty-two litres of diesel. I eat, drink and drive. I draw a line under this and turn it over to compose my message. Here it is.

I have decided to go to sleep soon and I know it will be difficult for you to wake me. My plan is to turn this boat upside down with the bow propped up on a low boulder, point it towards the setting sun and completely cover it with clumps of heather and gorse and grass. Then I will arrange stones from the beach all over it, positioning each one carefully so that they do not fall off. I will crawl into my chambered cairn, filling up the entrance behind me and I will lie down, wrapped in my blanket with all my treasures, which at the moment are: the plastic casing from a biro, a nearly empty half-bottle of whisky, a rapidly-dimming torch and a bunch of keys. Keys. A bunch of keys. A house key, an office key, a padlock key and a car key. Four silver keys lying in a pool of water at the bottom of this boat, beckoning like fairy lights.

It is a message from Klibreck.

I write in my best handwriting on the crushed receipt, just as the torch gives out: 'The chamber of my cairn is safe. Sorry. Better safe.'

My original message had been going to be lengthy and detailed but this seems to cover most of what I needed to say quite well. Once again I get out of the boat clutching my message and crawl about on the ground. I am looking for the Macallan bottle and I know that if I move every single stone on this beach I will eventually find it. I have found my purpose.

In the distance I can hear a car coming this way. It is coming to find me and it will take me home.

Angus Dunn

Animals
A set of short texts

The Mystery of the Heron

the stateliness of the heron is not lost
though it lies on the beach
wings spread
the small feathers of its breast
scattered
by the fox
who has eaten
what flesh
was on
its thin
body

The Cat

It must have come in earlier, when I left the door open to catch the last of the sunshine. Patches of its fur were missing and it was gaunt, bones showing through the skin. Its claws were yellow. It was yowling with its lips pulled back, a low, horrid sound. Its teeth were yellow too. It didn't belong in this house. Not in any house.

Keeping an eye on the cat, I moved slowly across to the window. Its back remained bent into a bow – only its head moved, watching me. I slid the bottom half of the window up, then edged round to the door, keeping well clear of the cat. It watched from the corner, every muscle tensed, still not moving, until the moment when I clapped my hands and yelled.

'Yaah!'

It leapt across the room and flung itself up at the window. The top half of the window. Its head whacked the window pane and as it fell back, the yellow claws caught on the wood. Its back legs scrabbled and it lunged against the glass once more, then again. And again, until it was exhausted and it just hung there. It was yowling, but the sound was more hopeless now than fierce.

I stood and watched. The cat hung there. Now and then it roused itself and scrabbled hopelessly, still trying to escape through the glass. Each time, its struggles shook the casement in its frame, so that the lower half of the window slowly slid shut under its weight.

Seagulls

I was lying on a hospital bed, looking at the wide lawns outside the window. A seagull was padding to and fro on the lawn, pecking now and then at the worms that came up.

I'd read about that trick, in a schoolbook. Supposedly the worms think the padding of feet is the sound of rain. But it was thrushes that did it, or blackbirds. Did the gulls learn it from them?

Didi's cafe was beside the dirt road that was the main street of Swayambhu. Sometimes monkeys would sit on the ridge of the corrugated iron roof.

I bought a slice of cake and took it to a table outside. I turned for one moment to draw in a chair. There was a thump on the table and when I turned, there was no cake. In a tree across the road, a monkey stood three-legged on a branch, looking at me, my cake in his other hand.

On the ferry to Skye, I climbed onto the upper deck, into the blustery wind. I took a bite from my sausage roll and turned to look at the sea. There was a thump on my hand and when I turned, there was no sausage roll.

High up already, a gull turned to look at me, tossed the sausage roll a little in its beak and swallowed it whole.

Sheep

For some reason that I can no longer completely understand, we always liked to go to the slaughter shed at Drumchork farm when they were killing the sheep. But the farm hands would never let us get close enough to see what was happening inside. We hung around at the edge of the pen, smelling the sheep and hearing their bleating.

The shed was only big enough for one beast at a time, each sheep being taken in its turn, and not coming out again. A slow business.

Decades later I notice, at last, that there must have been another door at the back.

Rabbit

Ben is in the push-chair, facing forwards. He is delighted by the rabbit at the roadside that doesn't run away. So am I, until I see that it is blind with myxomatosis. I walk on until the push-chair is safely past the rabbit.

Then, turning my back, I break the rabbit's neck and drop it over the fence into the long grass.

Not right away, but about a hundred yards further along the road, Ben tries to turn round in the safety straps. I lean over so that he can speak to me.

'You killed the rabbit.'

He has been thinking about it.

'Yes, I did.'

We walk on, both thinking.

Camel

It was not a sandy desert, like you see in films. It was a salty, stony desert, with gaunt shrubs that looked dead.

We had to drive past the camel every day – a wonder, at first. 'Look, a dead camel!'

Then it began to swell up, its belly a swollen hairy shape, as if it was pregnant. It began to stink and we all held our breath as we passed. The stomach grew ridiculously distended, its knobby spindly legs spreading apart in a disturbing parody of an invitation.

As we turned onto the main road each morning, the driver put his foot down hard and we all drew in a full breath. Sixty, seventy, eighty miles an hour, and we still had to breathe again before we were past the smell. Half a mile in each direction, the rotting camel reached out.

Then it began to deflate. After a weekend away, it seemed that the bulge was less tight, less round. The legs were the best indicator and we watched them carefully. Each day they were slightly less immodest.

One morning, we were talking in the car and the smell caught me by surprise. I had forgotten to hold my breath. When I looked for the camel on the way back, there was just a small tan hillock at the edge of the desert scrub.

And then one day, no-one could remember where it had been.

Three Short Texts

Beginning

His blonde hair is in dreadlocks and he is carrying a tent on his shoulder. He sways as he walks, as if he is still hearing music. He has camo trousers and a cheesecloth shirt that is hanging open.

She is wearing a long black gown with a white wool top. She is swinging two balls on strings as she walks, hips snaking to and fro as they whirl, her long brown hair moving in counterpoint.

He takes a long step across a ditch, onto the path through the woods.

She poises herself to jump, and her strings tangle. She takes a couple of seconds to unravel them, then makes the leap.

I lie on the hillside in the sunshine, watching them disappear among the trees.

Sometimes sunshine falls on them, sometimes they walk in shadow.

Face

I pointed at the doorstep. 'There was a bloodstain there for years, from when I smashed my knee off it. Look! Would you believe it? It's still there. That reddish patch.'

She bent down and looked at the broken corner of the doorstep.

'That's not a bloodstain,' she said. There was no malice in her voice. 'They've used river pebbles to make the concrete, and that's a broken piece of feldspar. Or possibly jasper.'

'Is it?' I knelt down to look. The irregular orange bloodstain was exactly as I remembered. I reached out and touched it. It was plainly just a stone. I could feel her, standing behind me, watching. Saying nothing.

I stood up and brushed my hands together.

'That's the kind of blood we had in *my* family.'

End

Pale yellow curtains covered the window, but they were alight from the sunshine and the room was full of light. Even the shadows in the room seemed to be made of paler, more insubstantial light.

As I put my card on the bedside table I brushed against the curtain, letting in a sudden spear of light. She opened her eyes and caught mine.

She was there, I could see it in her eyes. 'I thought you would be gone,' I said. I could not help smiling. 'But here you are, watching your own life, right to the very end.'

It seemed to me that her eyes were curious and pleased, as if seeing something quite unexpected and delightful.

What was it? What was she seeing when she looked at me?

I don't know. But it was good, I could feel it. I beamed at her as if we were two kids meeting in a play-park, while I spoke to her about whatever came to mind. About where she was, and why, and how good it was to see her.

The door opened and my sister's head came round the door.

'All right to come in?'

I nodded and kept talking. I had the card in my hand and I read it: 'My mother is a Ming vase. Ancient. Fragile. And precious.' I grinned. 'It was meant for your birthday, but I was in Edinburgh. Now you have it.'

I held her hand for a moment, then left the room. I looked up and down the corridor, finding the exit. A nurse was coming.

'Would you like to sit down for a while?'

'Sit down?' I said. 'I was just …'

She took my arm and led me to a lounge at the end of the corridor. 'There you are,' she said. 'Take your time.'

I went in and sat down. There was a box of tissues on the table, and a jug of water. Through the window I could see houses and the sea and, far off, cloud shadows on the sunny hillside. It was restful. I cried for a long time. It felt good.

John McGill

Aald Broon

There was a hatch between the kitchen and the dining room but Mother Dear never passed the food through it. She carried the laden plates out through the kitchen door and along the passageway and into the dining room; then she went back into the kitchen and watched us through the hatch while we ate. When she saw one of us tilting his plate to scoop up the last mouthful of soup, she shuffle-skipped back along the passageway and into the dining room and hovered.

Jeffrey, who was twelve when the cancer killed her and much more evil than Father or I, would slurp his soup fast to reach the final small puddle, then theatrically tilt his plate to bring her scurrying through. Then when she arrived at his shoulder he would settle the plate flat on the table again, drag his spoon idly through the dregs, laugh across at me and listen to her bones twitching.

Father ate slowly and never slurped. 'Why don't you sit down, dear?' he would say, nodding toward the empty place opposite his own. 'The soup is lovely.' And she would take one shuffling step in the direction of the empty chair and stop and say, 'No, I don't think so, dear, not today. I'll just have a little ...'

'When she hangs over my shoulder like that I can smell her Ritz Crackers,' Jeffrey said once, when we were alone. Savage to the end, he always kept his puddle of soup till last, after Father's final silent sip, while she twitched at his shoulder for agonies of minutes, dying in her bones. She would carry the dirty plates back through the passageway and bring us our main course and watch us through the hatch while she washed the soup plates – and again Jeffrey would bolt the food down and fetch her through and laugh at her twitching while he endlessly pursued a solitary recalcitrant pea.

Father chewed noiselessly, and you could see his eyebrows lift or his lips curl in a fleeting smile as he turned over phrases for next Sunday's sermon and fashioned long dry sentences for his many-chaptered book on John Knox. 'That was lovely, dear,' he would tell her as she collected the plates. 'I hope you're having some too.' She would frown for three seconds, considering, before she replied. 'I'm all right, dear, I've had a little ...'

Then she would be in the frame of the hatch nibbling her Ritz Crackers and watching us while we ate the pudding; and not till it was all over, the last bowl collected and washed and dried and stacked in the cupboard, would she sit down for her half-hour with the Church Times and let her bones settle.

Marjorie. Believe me, believe me, I have to pause and think before I can recall Mother Dear's name, and I sincerely forget whether, before she married Father, she was a Robertson or a Robinson or a Robson.

She had wonderful small expert teeth. One Youth Fellowship Fun Evening she demonstrated how to make a map of Scotland from a McVitie's Digestive biscuit, starting in the east with the easy curves of the Moray Firth and the Firth of Forth, then nibbling counter-clockwise around Cape Wrath and in-and-out up-and-down through the glorious intricacies of the west coast. 'It's such a pity you can't do the islands,' she said, blushing scarlet at our applause. 'I love Mull.'

As a girl she had been an athlete of some note, and there were cups and medals of assorted hue gathering dust in cupboards all over the house, but once she gave up eating anything but Ritz Crackers and the occasional McVitie's Digestive she grew so thin that she could never find clothes to fit, and her stockings were chronically wrinkled.

I think she liked me better than Jeffrey because I lacked his wit and his wickedness, and because for the couple of years before he was born I was her chief joy and there was enough flesh on her bones to let her sit me on her lap and put her arm around me without danger of bruising to either of us. Somewhere I remember those three years, but not in my head.

I was absurdly too old, eight or nine I think, when she gave me Old Brown; but she knew it would have to be me or nobody, because Jeffrey, even at six, would have laughed. She had been sifting jumble for the Spring Bazaar and had thrown him into the Not Quite Good Enough pile, a sizable heap because Father insisted on quality, even for jumble and junk.

'But I just couldn't bring myself to throw him away,' she said. 'He was lying there and his arms were reaching up and he looked so ...'

'Yes, dear,' Father said.

'I looked down at him and he looked up at me and he was ...'

Father raised his eyebrows and Jeffrey laughed. Mother wanted to talk about a Christmas card with a painting by Hugo van der Goes but Father couldn't remember it and never liked wasting words on popish things anyway. I remembered the card because she had shown me it especially, so she passed Old Brown to me.

'You can look after him for me, Giles,' she said, ignoring Father's deepening frown and Jeffrey's swelling laughter.

It was age that marked him out for the Not Quite Good Enough pile: he was worn all over to a fine latticework of thread – a bear without fur. But he had two ears and two scowling eyes and four movable limbs and a grey nose and a sad smile that now and again verged on the sardonic. He was nearly a yard long and filled my arms when I took him from Mother Dear, and I could see Father out of focus in the corner of my eye wrinkling his nose and clearly thinking the whole thing was unsanitary and vaguely popish, and I held my breath waiting for him to say, 'Don't be silly, dear, he'll have to go in the bin.'

But he didn't say it. He went into the garden to plant the lettuces, and Jeffrey went to help him, still laughing.

Mother Dear had long since stopped hugging me by then and she couldn't have been hugging Father either, because he was a big prop forward and would have broken her in two. Father and Jeffrey loved to wrestle in the garden but I never liked rough games. Old Brown was horribly scratchy, but he immediately supplanted all my other bedmates and my cheek was usually red in the morning from rubbing on his threadbare belly.

He stayed with me. Father's book got longer and Mother Dear watched us from her hatch and her teeth fell out and her breath began to smell bad and on the prize-giving day when Jeffrey won a lot of things for being dux of his primary school she died. They put her six-and-a-half stone in a coffin and she lay anxiously smiling for three days in the parlour of the manse. They buried her on a Friday, and on the following Sunday Father gave a bright beautiful peach of a sermon that brought tears even to his own eyes and stopped the paper-crinklers and the sherbet-lemon suckers dead in their tracks, sniffling in every pew. The night of the funeral I didn't cry, but I had a pain in the back of my head and a sickness in my stomach and I slept with Old Brown's left ear clenched hard in my teeth and woke with the headache gone but a bad sour taste in my mouth.

I wasn't a high-flier like Jeffrey, and Father was always a little embarrassed when people asked about me, especially since I was such a good cook and liked doing the housework. But I coped well enough – an 'A' in History and 'B's in my three other Highers – and in the end wasn't far off a First, or so Professor Armstrong told me, in a fairly brilliant Year at Aberdeen. Old Brown stayed with me all through the four years and through the year of Training College and if the truth be told, he was the only one who ever shared my bed the whole night long. There were one or two near-misses, of course, and because it was the time when girls were discovering they were allowed to like it as well and many of them were becoming quite aggressive, I was able to lose my virginity in a gradual sort of way.

The nearest miss was with Sandra. I've never really recovered from it. We had already gone most of the way – all of it, in fact, as far as my knowledge of the thing was concerned – once or twice at her bedsit, and sleeping together at least till daybreak seemed the obvious next thing. So we sneaked into my flat, which I shared with a divinity student, at midnight one Friday, tiptoeing past his door, hand-in-hand and giggling. It was the most romantic night of my life. We sipped two glasses of Valpollicella each and Sandra had some puffs from a joint and the smell of it made me nervous but excited as well, then she fell back on the bed and I fell on top of her, even though the lights were still on, and the next thing, just as I was about to kiss her, just as I was closing my eyes for the first thrilling touch of lips, she screamed. I thought I'd hurt her and jumped off the bed and she jumped up after me, shaking all over and looking as if she might scream again. But then I saw the bulge in the quilt and realised what it was, and peeled the quilt back and pulled him out.

'It's all right,' I said. 'He lives here.'

And that wasn't as bad as you might think; it wasn't the disaster it could have been, because Sandra was a nice, nice girl and she thought it was sweet that a grown lad like me (I never reached Father's six-foot-one or came near his fifteen stone, but I was fairly well-developed, not out of place wearing Aran sweaters and singing Irish folksongs in the Students' Union) should still be taking his teddy bear to bed with him. So if anything it was a good thing; it broke the ice quite well, and she started kissing me in a nice, Friday-night feathery sort of way, and biting my earlobes, and loosening my shirt-buttons, and we both got aroused and rolled over so that I was on top and beginning to pay her back with some of the same treatment. But then, while I was kissing her and thinking about her buttons, she starting giggling, laughing so hard she had us both shaking and the bed creaking so much I thought it was bound to wake the divinity student. Coming on top of the other thing, the scream, it finished me. I sat up on the bed and she knew right away I was hurt.

'I'm sorry,' she said, sitting up and putting her hand on my arm. 'It was that thing, I just caught a glimpse of it.' She nodded toward my bedside locker. I had propped Old Brown against the lamp and he was sitting there crouched forward with his hands on his knees, staring at us.

'I just saw his face, upside-down, and it looked so funny,' she said.

'Mm,' I said.

She tried to get the mood back. 'Look at his face. He's got such a funny expression; he looks so cross.'

'He's jealous,' I said. I said it bitterly, and she heard it and squeezed my hand.

'Don't be upset.'

'I'm not,' I lied.

'I didn't mean to laugh. I just got a shock, seeing his face.'

She started kissing me again but I couldn't respond: it was all I could do not to shrug her off. She was a nice girl and she didn't blame me or act offended like most other girls would have done. She said she would like to spend the night, like to be with me, even if we didn't, but I said I'd rather she went home, I had a touch of 'flu anyway. She left and there were tears in her eyes and I turned back from kissing her cheek and went into the room and grabbed Old Brown by the left leg and swung him over my head and beat him up and down again and again and again on my pillow. Then I threw him across the room but he landed propped against the wall fixing me with his usual disapproving scowl, and I went over and picked him up and he slept as he always did with his head on the pillow beside mine.

College finished and I got a job in a good department in a good school in the north, and a place in the boys' hostel rent-free in exchange for a few evenings supervision duty. Old Brown came with me, because I couldn't think what else to do with him. The boys found out about him but by the time that happened I had whacked all of them at ping-pong (that was the one success Father had had in making a man of me) and shown them a thing or two on the parallel bars, and my credit was high, so nobody laughed. Not to my face, anyway. They called him Aald Broon and he became a standing joke.

Girls, of course, were out of the question, but I wasn't too upset by that. The thing with Sandra had got to me, and I felt I needed a bit of time and a bit of space in which to work things out: to get myself orientated, if you know what I mean. Sometimes the younger boys asked me to bring Aald Broon down to the common room and I would sit him on my knee and do a few ventriloquist's tricks. Crude, but funny enough to make them laugh and comfort them on a cold winter's night with their mothers and fathers miles away on far-flung islands.

They liked me – everybody, I mean. The older teachers shook their heads and frowned a bit and said, 'Oh, these modern methods,' but they liked me, and the women saw I was just a boy a long way from home and mothered me a bit. As for the pupils, well, Aald Broon and I became a bit of a team to them, and they treated me just like one of themselves, really. But they were always properly respectful, never too familiar. So it was natural enough, when the headmaster came back from a course about how to be a Modern Headmaster and decided Morning Assemblies should be upgraded and revitalized a bit, that he should ask me if I might want to lead one. I jumped at the chance, of course, and he laughed and said I should strum a few chords on my guitar – and, the assembly being March-the-somethingth, I might want to say a word or two about Mother's Day.

Mother's Day. I thought and thought and all I could see was her little frightened head framed in the hatch and all I could hear was the small suppressed whimper of frustration she used to make when Jeffrey lowered his soup-plate back to the table and started to dabble his spoon in the last puddle, and all I could smell was the mingling of fear and Ritz Crackers on her breath.

I wanted to talk to them about killing and capitalism and Afghanistan and Iraq.

The Monday came, a fine spring morning, and I was more than ready. My one worry was how I could fit it all into the fifteen minutes I was allowed – Mother's Day and capitalism and Afghanistan and Iraq and a strum on the guitar and, because they would have expected it, a bit of a caper with Aald Broon.

I started with a song – always good for shock value. I sat on the edge of the stage with a desk behind me and strummed and gave them 'Johnny I Hardly Knew Ye,' laying on the pathos thick as Guinness on the final chorus till they were sniffling in their seats – even the boys. Then I flashed up a picture of an Iraqi mother with a dead baby in her arms and talked about Mother's Day and that took me to mothers in general and that led on to my own mother and the hatch and the Ritz Crackers and her bones and Aald Broon, her gift to me. The bell rang but I carried on and they were too polite to stop me. I took Aald Broon from the floor of the stage where I had laid him and bent his legs and sat him on the desk and told them I was going to kill him and chop him in pieces and disembowel him right there in front of their eyes. A lot of people laughed, not quite knowing what else they could do, but they stopped and the hall was thick with silence when I brought out the knife and the chopper from the hostel kitchen and there was a collective gasp when I raised the knife in both hands above my head and shouted, 'Now, now, now, now you'll see!' and drove it down into Aald Broon's fat hairless belly so hard it went all the way through and stuck in the desk. Then some of them were screaming and I was chopping his legs and arms off and throwing them into the hall and jumping on my guitar, smashing it to matchwood. In the end, while the young ones howled and hugged each other in their fright, I took the torso from the desk and pushed my fingers into the hole the knife had made and ripped the stuffing out of him and stamped it into the stage. I stamped and stamped until somebody – a PE teacher, they told me later – pinned my arms to my side and lifted me up and carried me off the stage to the front row seats. I was crying, and the place was in uproar.

The Director wants to sack me and the Headmaster isn't sure and the parents are up in arms and the man from the union says if I plead a sudden death in the family and a bit of a viral infection he'll be able to get me off with a written warning. Two little white lies, he says, and I'll be okay. He doesn't want to hear what I have to say about Mother's Day; he says I've to have a rest and forget it all and quite soon it will just be an island joke. That I'll be a deputy headmaster and famous – the man who murdered a teddy bear in front of eight hundred and twenty-six witnesses.

Pam Beasant

The Anniversary

His death formed in her gut like a stone;
an obstruction she learned to by-pass
putting off the operation.

Its rough, heavy presence blocked all paths
to him, made no demands except to
let it lie there. The day came when she

reached in, unplugged her own gut, held his
death, extracted, in her living hands.
Grief, like arterial flow, glutted

the breach, unstemmed. No comfort; except
the part of him inside that patches
her will stay, grafted on the tissue

to make it heal, and the stone, shut tight
in a drawer will be accessible,
benign; all the sharp surfaces smoothed

by her intricate imprint.

How long does it take to write a poem?

MacCaig, wily old master,
trotted out the unvarying reply:
two fags.
It always drew a laugh.
He meant
don't over or underplay the art.
Don't make it god.
But his eyes –
Suilven pools smarting in a Rose St pub –
betrayed the devotion of a life spent
watching, smoking,
filling volumes.

Winter Dawn

Two tides, smelling like ozone,
chop cross-ways against the pier.

The *Graemsay* glides out,
slows through the Sound on the swell.

Light breaks on her wake –
a scattering benediction.

Flash of a wing-tip on the quarrelling tides,
a cat, paused by a creel, slips by.

Home before sun reaches cold stone,
body scrubbed raw for the day.

Land/Mind

Landscape, satisfying word,
hard-edged, mobile, varied, green.
Mindscape is silvered, dangerous,
too vast and fleeting. Milton's hell
exhaling from a mouth long dead.

Patterns extracted from the land,
hay stacks, fence posts, standing stones,
thread the air;
mind mosaics are mist-edged,
time hissing through gaps.

Betrayal

What's the core of a life? Is it
to think you are something,
or have something? Or is it not
to know – to find it
with new coordinates each time?

The view from a window; the way
light plays on the land,
or the way you see it, can change;
life's map gone awry,
monsters outlined among the gaps.

How can love lie – what does its true
taint look like? Is it
visible – like outlines? What does
its removal leave
behind? (Are questions the one truth?)

Love, a trammelled, mire-sodden thing,
can gather in a
ball of dirt; be hurled in one
brutal parting blow.
Betrayal, worse than a clean wound

can maim or kill; or set you free
on a strange map – stark, brave and new.

Pam Beasant

Running with a Snow Leopard

Eye to eye through the wire fence,
no surface in the long, connecting silence.
Your arm moves a fraction, the leopard
flicks his tail.

Suddenly you run the fence's length
like a young wind. He follows,
full throttle, veering closer,
mirroring the ecstasy.

He crouches ready to spring.
You copy. Both
brimful of dangerous joy
prepare to meet.

The fence looks suddenly low.
Reaching out, fearful,
I capture you back,
to the lesser, leopard-less world.

You match a lithe pace to mine,
nature reinstated;
but in your glance back at the animal,
I catch naked collusion.

Joanna Ramsey

The Long View

Ella slipped off her rings and left them lying on the table beside Gwen's unfinished mug of tea, fearing to lose them out on the hill. After the unfailing greyness of a long northern winter, daffodils curved in bright moving swathes below the garden wall.

She heard voices, and Sophie, her daughter, came into the kitchen, tucking her long hair behind her ears and laughing, jostling her cousin Beth in the aftermath of some private tease.

'Where's Mum?' Beth asked.

'She's gone ahead to check that everything's there.'

'Again!'

'She just wants it done right. You know what Gwen's like.'

Sophie flicked the kettle switch and spooned coffee into mugs.

'Want one, Beth?'

'Is there time?'

'We've got the whole day.'

'No, we haven't,' said Ella. 'Four hundred young trees to plant, and a funeral this afternoon.'

'Are you going to the funeral, Mum?' asked Sophie.

'I'm not sure.'

I should go, Ella thought, rubbing protective lotion into her ringless hands. I ought to pay my respects, even though I hardly knew the woman. It was not unknown for the entire population of the island to turn out for a funeral. But the thought of putting on a dark dress and encasing her legs in unaccustomed tights made Ella shudder a little. She could see that out on the hill the sun was shining, and she left the girls to their coffee and began to climb the path towards Gwen's stooping figure, calling a greeting as she drew nearer.

They had been sisters-in-law and neighbours for many years and were comfortable with one another, an undemonstrative affection having grown between them. Gwen looked round at Ella now.

'I'm just checking these bags of saplings. I hope they haven't got too dry.'

92

She peered into another plastic sack. 'We ought to get them in today, for sure. You are up to this, aren't you, Ella?'

'Of course. I'm fine.'

They were slow to get started; it was almost mid-morning before the planting began in earnest. Gwen and Tom's son, Alistair, did not appear, and Tom and Brian were a long time checking the ewes. Everything needed for the tree-planting had to be carried or dragged up to the edge of the field, and the slope was steep. Beth and Sophie came struggling up with the spades Gwen had set out in the yard, but they had forgotten hammers and had to go back.

'Alistair's left a message,' Beth said breathlessly, as she dropped the hammers onto the grass, narrowly missing her own feet. 'He says he won't be up until later, if at all. Helen got roped in to do sandwiches for the funeral tea, so he's had to drive her down there, and the girls aren't even dressed yet. And Sarah's had a nosebleed all over her bed.'

Gwen sighed and shook her head. 'Come on Ella, we'll get the rest of the stuff ourselves.'

But the wooden stakes for the new trees were awkward to lug, tied loosely in large bundles which banged against everyone's legs. Gwen went back down again for the flasks of tea that had been left behind in Ella's kitchen.

'I'll go,' she said. 'You look fairly exhausted already, Ella, and we've not even begun yet.'

Ella sat on the grass to wait for Gwen and looked out to sea. In spite of the hard work ahead, the day had a holiday feel to it. This was all Gwen's idea: to get involved with a local project to re-establish areas of native species, and to plant small areas of woodland in a landscape which was all but treeless. She had got everyone interested, suggested sites, filled in grant applications and made the necessary calls. Now she was coming back up the hill at an energetic pace.

'Off we go then,' she said, putting the flasks down carefully in the long grass beside the new fence. 'Tom and Brian'll be here in a wee minute.'

Ella thrust her spade through the matted grass to make the first cuts, as Gwen had shown her. She prised a tiny sapling from the cluster beside her and slipped it into the notch of moist earth, treading the turf down around it. Next she spread out a mulch mat and eased the opening over the birch's delicate buds, weighting the black plastic with a stone, against the lift of the slight breeze, which was almost constant on the hillside. Then she shoved in her spade again, feeling the suck of the peaty soil, tucking the mat in tightly to keep out weeds.

'Stake next,' prompted Gwen, handing her one. Ella hammered hard and then slid the shelter down, trying not to knock off the precious new growth.

'First one done!' she said, pulling the ties firmly. Looking up, she saw Gwen starting her second. The girls were working more slowly, helping each other, and when Brian and Tom arrived they went to labour higher up the slope, on the more difficult stony ground near the burn.

They planted steadily. It was wonderful to have such luck with the weather. The cloud was high and unthreatening, and the sea pulsed quietly into the bay. The sun had more warmth than Ella had expected, and she stopped after her fourth tree to shed a layer. Gwen, digging nearby, paused to look at her as she shrugged off her thick sweater.

'You've lost weight, Ella. There'll be nothing of you. Not that hip and thigh diet again, is it?'

'Heavens, no. Haven't done that for years. Put me off broccoli for ever.'

They stopped for a cup of thermos tea. Gwen had sugared it for the men, and the girls wouldn't drink it. Ella subsided onto the grass, grateful for a rest, and Brian came to sit beside her, giving her his slow smile. A man of few words, he moved unhurriedly through life.

'How long will it take for them to grow into proper trees, then?' asked Beth. She spoke with the plaintive impatience of a child who can't wait to see her baking come out of the oven, and Gwen caught Ella's eye, trying not to laugh.

'In twenty years we'll have some fair-sized trees,' Gwen said. 'You know what this climate's like. We'll lose a few on the seaward side, but it's good soil here.'

'I'll be nearly forty!' Beth looked bemused.

'That doesn't seem very long, really,' Sophie said thoughtfully. 'I thought Aunt Gwen was going to say fifty years or so.'

'They'll never be very tall,' Brian told them. 'But our grandfather planted those trees by the burn, didn't he, Tom?'

'Aye, that's right enough. Maybe a hundred years ago now. Took cuttings from those trees beside Lindale and set them in.' He pointed to a huddle of willows bearing soft grey buds, and rowans which looked as if they had always been in that place, their mossy roots bedded amongst the stones at the edge of the falling water. 'And he wrote it all down in a book, wee notes and sketches. Did I never show it to you, Beth?'

It was good, Ella thought, to take the long view. To start something that would remain always, after you had gone, and even after your children had gone.

'What on earth – ? Look, down by Billy's cottage!'

Sophie had jumped to her feet and was pointing. They all looked. Gwen stood up. Three figures, one large and two very small, were running across one of the lower fields. A process of elimination identified them as Alistair and his two daughters.

'What the heck are they doing?' grumbled Tom. 'I thought he'd be up here by now. He's got no business to be running about the fields.'

But Beth's sharp young eyes had detected another movement. 'It's the ram! It's jumped the fence again, I'll bet.'

The figures became more clearly etched as they dashed onto the tarmac of the single-track road in pursuit of the errant ram. It darted ahead, stopped and waited provocatively as Alistair and his girls approached it, and then scrambled across the ditch onto the open sand dunes. Its pursuers disappeared behind the grassy mounds. The watchers on the hillside stared hopefully, but there was no more excitement to be had for the moment. After a few minutes they went on with the planting. Ella felt she was working more slowly than the others, but she needed to stop every now and then to catch her breath and wipe the dampness from her brow.

She straightened up, feeling a dull ache spread across her shoulders. Gwen came past for another sack of tree shelters, and stood for a moment beside Ella, looking out to sea. The mainland, which earlier had been masked with a gauze of mist, was beginning to show more clearly on the skyline, and the shimmer of light on the calm water was almost too bright.

'Don't tire yourself, Ella,' Gwen said. 'I know I wanted it all done today, but Tom and I could finish off tomorrow if need be. You don't want to make yourself ill again. You've not been right this year.'

Ella smiled and shook her head. 'I'll be fine. I'm just a wee bit weary.'

She scanned the valley. She saw someone come out of the bothy and walk toward the beach. She saw the English woman from the holiday cottage peg washing on a line, the clothes hanging almost motionless in the warm air. These people moved below, oblivious to her attention. The valley was reduced to essentials: road and field and slope, and beyond them, the water. The small beauties were lost: the texture of grasses, the spreading patches of spring wildflowers, the contrasting tones of oystercatchers against the new green of pasture. All were smoothed away and absorbed by distance. Sometimes voices or the sound of an engine drifted up.

She looked for the postman's van, but it was far too early, and the only vehicle she could see was a white four-wheel-drive she had seen parked by the hostel that morning. As she watched, it sped smoothly along the winding road towards the shore.

'Tourists,' Tom said, following the direction of her gaze. 'Met them in the pub last night.'

'They seem to be going to Angus Buchan's place.'

Tom stopped tucking in a mulch mat, to have another look. 'They'll have taken the wrong turn. They'll be wanting the beach.'

The road to the beach forked, and the signpost, blown down in a gale several winters ago, had never been replaced. Sure enough, a minute later, Ella saw the white vehicle stop and begin to reverse. Too fast, she thought, slightly alarmed, wanting to shout at them to slow down. Up here, high above the valley, watching the almost soundless activity, she had a curious sense of omniscience and power.

I wonder if God feels like this, she thought. It's as if I could just touch them with a finger, one little push and – oh Lord! She gasped, horrified. The car had tilted and lay at an angle in the ditch. I didn't do it, she wanted to cry.

Tom was already running down the field. Gwen looked up to see what was wrong.

'They're getting out, Tom!' she yelled after him. 'I don't think they're hurt.'

Four figures emerged from the stranded vehicle and stood in the middle of the road. Ella could see them gesticulating, arms rising and falling. Another person ran out of a nearby cottage and went towards them.

'There's Nina,' said Gwen, relieved. 'She's spotted them. Angus too, probably.'

Tom had stopped, halfway down the slope, waiting to see what would happen next. A few moments later, a tractor trundled out from behind a farm building further along the shore road. Ella could hear the faint burr of the tractor's engine as Angus chugged towards the tourists. She saw him climb down, with something slung over his shoulder that might have been a coil of rope.

'He'll sort it,' Tom said, coming back up, puffing heavily. 'Blooming idiots. Come on, let's get these trees in.'

Ella began again, finding the earth softer and easier to dig as she worked her way down the slope. They planted downy birch and rowan, with grey willows at the edge, leaving spaces for wild roses to be put in at the end of the summer. Months before we need to do that, Ella thought. She leaned on her spade, sick for a second with inexpressible fear.

'Once we get the blood test results,' Dr Allen had said, 'we'll have a clearer idea of what's ahead. But in the meantime, you have to talk to Brian and Sophie. Gwen too. You need their support. You know you do. Or do you want me to tell them?'

'Are you all right, Mum?' Sophie asked, coming past with an armful of stakes.

'Just a bit tired, my love.'

They didn't talk much as they worked. The planting had a rhythm to it, and they moved up and down the field quietly, absorbed in what they were doing, the peace of the day broken only by the pounding of hammers on stakes. Brian smiled as he passed Ella, nodding his approval when he saw how much she had done. It was the island way to be reticent, and he and Ella had long ago fallen into the habit of wordless communication. Now, confronted with a crisis, Ella bucked against this native reserve and stoicism. I would give anything, she realised, for a soothing salve of words, for reassuring phrases.

But first she had to tell him.

'Lunch break!' yelled Gwen. Ella laid down her spade thankfully. Beyond the burn there was a long, low dwelling, derelict for years but recently re-roofed with stone slabs. Gwen had lugged a gas cylinder and a small stove across from her own house, and set a pan of soup to heat. They all sat outside and drank from paper cups, burning their mouths and fingers, and Sophie and Beth went round with plastic boxes full of sandwiches. Ella was pleased when Sophie came to sit next to her, and rested her head for a moment on Ella's shoulder.

'It's a funny way to spend your holiday,' Ella said to her, lightly kissing her hair. 'But it's good to have your help, my love.'

'Oh, don't worry, I'm enjoying myself!'

After a moment or two of silence, Sophie reached across and touched

Ella's hand.

'Mum – you're not wearing your wedding ring.'

'No, I took it off and left it at home. And Nan's ring. I was afraid of losing them when I was digging.'

Her wedding ring was too loose, for the first time ever, but Sophie accepted the reply without question. Ella cast a glance at her daughter: at the light on her hair, the curve of her cheek. Did everyone else see how beautiful she was? So young and full of potential, poised on the rim of the nest, ready to soar high?

Oh God, spare me from sentimentality, Ella prayed. Spare me. Just spare me. Oh God, oh God.

'Egg sandwich?' Tom bent over her with the plastic box, doing the rounds. The egg smelt unpleasant after being shut in the box all morning. Ella shook her head.

'No thanks, Tom.'

Brian took two and balanced them on a large flat stone. They saw Robert, one of their neighbours, coming up the slope towards them.

'What like?' he called, in the familiar island greeting. 'Any soup left? Thanks, Gwen, that's grand. Did you see the drama going on down there a wee while ago, Tom?'

'What, the tourists in the ditch? Aye. Nobody hurt?'

'Just the car. A wee dent, that's all. They're pleasant folk, Angus says. I hear you were speaking to them in the pub last night.' He tilted back his head to swig the last of Gwen's lentil soup, the paper cup almost crushed in his huge and powerful hand.

'What do you think of my fences, then?'

'Just grand, Robert,' Brian said. 'You've made a right fine job of them.'

'They should keep the sheep away from the trees. I don't know about rabbits. Nothing seems to keep rabbits out. Has the grant come through all right?'

'Aye, it's all in hand.'

Gwen stood up and began collecting cups. 'Let's press on. We've done well so far.'

They worked into the early afternoon. Cloud drifted across with a faint promise of rain, but later the sun reasserted itself and warmth spread over the hill again. More and more of the slope was covered with tiny trees and black squares of matting. Sophie and Beth were flagging, talking more and planting less. Even Gwen was slowing down, glancing at her watch more frequently. With a sinking heart, Ella remembered the funeral. As if reading her mind, Brian leaned his spade against the fence.

'That's me done for today. I need to go and get changed. Are you coming, Tom? Gwen?' He knew Ella didn't want to go, and he wasn't going to put any pressure on her.

'Aye, we'll both be along.'

'What about you, Ella?' Gwen asked. 'What did you decide?'

'I ought to come,' Ella said slowly, 'but I don't think I will. Do you think her family will mind? I didn't know her well.'

The thought of the funeral service and, worse, the tea-party afterwards in the chilly hall, filled her with dread.

'Of course they won't mind,' Gwen said kindly. 'I'll tell them you were needed here. You keep an eye on these two.' She nodded towards Sophie and Beth.

'I'll see you later, love,' said Brian, as he gathered up his tools.

She watched him head down the hill towards their house, before she made the effort to put in six more rowans. Her entire body was aching now with fatigue. The girls were comparing blisters on their young, unhardened palms.

'I don't think I can do much more,' Ella said to them. 'I'm going to have a rest before I clear up.'

She went across to the fence, where Gwen had left the thermos flasks, to see if there was any more tea. Her mouth felt dry and she was dizzy. The light on the water dazzled her and she turned away from it, looking inland.

After a while, she saw what she had been waiting for. The post van appeared, in the dip where the road to the ferry struck between two hills. It moved soundlessly towards the straggle of houses, stopping first at the post box. Young Ben, the postman, whom she had known since he was born, got out. He was too far away for her to see him clearly, but she knew he would unlock the box, remove a handful of letters and stow them in the van. She watched him get back in, and the van began to move again. Her heart was thudding as he stopped at the top of their track. She knew that he would have a letter for her today, because Dr Allen had telephoned last night to tell her. It would be a long manilla envelope, forwarded from the surgery, with her plane ticket to the mainland in it.

'You'll need chemotherapy,' Dr Allen had said. 'You'll have to go to Aberdeen. You might be away for quite a while. You do understand that, don't you, Ella?'

'There's Ben with the post,' she called to the girls. 'I think I'll go down.'

But Ben was coming up, to find them. She saw his young, smiling face and the stride of his healthy limbs; surely he was no harbinger of death. Beth was looking too, and running her hands through her dark, curly hair, suddenly self-conscious.

'Fine day!' Ben greeted them, climbing over the stile. Sophie whispered something in Beth's ear, and they both nodded their heads at him.

'A letter for you, Mrs Harcus,' said Ben, holding it out. His eyes were mild and innocent. 'I thought I'd bring it up and see how you were getting on. You've been doing a grand job here.' His eyes took in the triangle of field planted with saplings, and slid round to Sophie and Beth.

Ella reached out her hand and took the letter. 'Thank you, Ben.' She folded it over and pushed it deep into the pocket of her trousers.

'I've a message for you, too,' Ben remembered. 'Mum said to tell you the concert's fixed for the first week in July. She's looking for volunteers to help with the supper afterwards.'

'July? That's a long way off yet,' Ella said, too brusquely.

'Aye, it's a fair while, I suppose.' He sounded apologetic. Ella rebuked herself: don't shoot the messenger.

'Are you off soon?' Ben asked, turning to Sophie and Beth. He addressed the question to both of them, but his eyes kept straying to Beth's face.

'The early boat on Saturday,' Sophie answered cheerfully, looking forward to getting back to college in spite of her enjoyment in being at home. 'My term starts on Monday. Beth's too.'

'You'll miss the end of the lambing, then?' he said. 'That's a pity.'

'We'll be back again before you know it,' Beth said, in a gentle way. 'Home for two months in the summer.'

Oh, island life, thought Ella. Always somebody going away. The tearing of ties. So painful for those left behind. But she wanted more than this for Sophie: a wider horizon, bigger chances, the kind of choices she herself had been able to make. But one must always be able to come back. To leave the island for ever was unthinkable, incomer though she might be. She had grown into the place and belonged to it now.

'You'll have to keep coming back, anyway,' Ben was saying, looking directly at Beth this time. 'To see how your trees are getting on.'

'Aye, of course I will.' Beth smiled at him. 'But they'll grow fine. I'll be bringing my children up here one day, to pick pussy willow buds. And my grandchildren. You'll see.' She knew Ben could be her future if she wanted, and she gazed at him quizzically, tossing back the dark mass of her hair.

So young, yet so confident, so certain she seemed. Taking the long view. Sophie had this optimism too, and it comforted Ella. But as she turned her head she saw Tom's car. Moving slowly down the track below them, on its way to the funeral.

Elyse Jamieson

Peyton and Lewis Tailoring

My wife's waiting for me outside. I don't have long. She's always there, with a meal on the table, or an outfit to opinionate on. 'You're a tailor, Jim!' she yells. 'You know what you're talking about! Do I look good!?' She's stunning and impatient, and I love her. Yet I'm not in love with her. I couldn't live without her but I can barely live with her.

I came out when I was fifteen. My parents disowned me, and I left school at sixteen. Jim's been looking after me ever since. Him and Margaret, they're not like parents to me, but they were always there. He taught me everything I needed to know about being a tailor, and now I'm one of the best in London. I owed him a lot, and I promised myself I'd repay him.

Andy's a fantastic guy. He's smart, charming and good-looking. We've cared for him since he was just a boy. We didn't adopt him; he wouldn't let us. I guess I'm sort of glad that we didn't. I treated him like a son and he treated me like a father. But we both knew that wasn't true.

For my twenty-fifth birthday, Jim gave me a share in the business. **Peyton and Lewis Tailors,** *it became. Margaret baked a cake too. Awfully good, it was. Light and spongy. I was almost more excited by it than I was by the partnership! No, that's a lie. I'm sorry, you told me not to do that. Really, I apologise. Yes, let's move on ...*

I started teaching him the tricks of the trade when he was seventeen. After only a year, he was amazing. Almost better than me! But I waited until his twenty-fifth birthday to offer him a share. I needed to know he could be trusted, and these things take time. What happened in those eight years? Not a lot! Can we speed this up please? I'm in a bit of a rush. Well, okay. I was thirty-three when I first met him, forty-two when I handed over a part of my enterprise ...

I was so proud. After everything my parents had said – about how being gay would mean no-one would want me, about how telling people I preferred other men would make them judge me – I was a partner in a highly successful tailoring business. I guessed the public might judge me if they knew. But they didn't have to know. Jim was fine with it, anyway. I understand why now. And besides, I'm not a pervert. I never even thought along those lines.

Yes, I knew he was homosexual when I took him on. Obviously I realised what other people would say, but I could see that he was honest. And reliable. Andy was always reliable, y'know. That was something I liked about him from the start. I knew he'd make a good partner for me someday ... No! Not like that! It didn't ... It wasn't meant to ... Are you sure? All right. I'm very sorry. Shall I continue?

That first year was a good year, and it never really went downhill. We signed contracts with many different figures in society, each more important than the last. Top government associates wanted us to make suits for worldwide conferences, and celebrities needed our designs for the red carpet. Working as a part of that was amazing. I'll never forget my name being in **OK** *and* **Hello!** *magazines. 'Andy Lewis, stylist to the stars,' it said. Clichéd, it's true – and yet so memorable.*

Andy brought a whole new life to the business. We evolved into this modern machine – we even branched out into designing. Somehow, I'm still not exactly sure how, the press got wind of his ... being gay. And yet no-one cared; it was nothing to be ashamed of. His parents never contacted him, poor thing. It was just after that that I began to think of him differently, y'know? I'd never thought of anyone else like that since I'd met Maggie. Especially not a man! It's unheard of! Taboo, even!

Jim started acting ... I dunno. Differently. There was nothing wrong with the way he was; he just wasn't the Jim I knew. I didn't ask questions, though. A rough patch with Margaret, that was my theory. I suppose in a way I was right. Why didn't I ask questions? Because I didn't believe that it was my business. You wouldn't ask your boss about his relationships, would you? Oh, whatever. You're a shrink.

I think Andy noticed, but he never said a thing. Too polite, that guy. He was thirty-six, thirty-seven by that point. Ten years go by really quickly when you're on top, y'know? We'd designed and fitted for hundreds of clients. There was a point where I almost stopped falling in love with him: it was our silver wedding anniversary. We went to Vienna, and it was amazing. Have you ever been? No? Oh, if you do go, you really should visit St Stephen's Cathedral …

He sort of went back to normal after that. I could see that there was still something bugging him, but I tried not to let it bother me. Of course I cared about him. He was like a father figure to me. Someone you admire; aspire to be like. An idol, if you will.

… And there were all these cafés. We spent our days drinking coffee and our nights dancing. Meanwhile? Meanwhile Andy stayed back here and single-handedly ran the business. We were away for three weeks, and in that time we gained more clients than we had ever had before. I sort of thought about packing it all in, y'know? Handing over the whole thing to him. But I decided I was too young to retire. I mean, fifty-five? No.

No. I was never attracted to him.

It was inevitable, really. Andy met someone and they started going out quite regularly. Damien Voss. He came over to dinner a few times, and he was an all right guy. They were seeing each other for a while, actually. Nearly a year, I'd say. They got closer and I became steadily more jealous.

Then there was Damien. We were together eleven months. It'd been my first relationship in some time. Yes, despite the fact I was an almost-celebrity, no-one wanted to be with me. Not even for a quickie and then get your name in **Heat** *magazine. No, I couldn't quite believe it either.*

But suddenly they finished with each other. Andy stopped going out on Friday nights, and Damien was never mentioned again. I never did find out why. I guess he was cheating on our Andy. It happens. I didn't ask questions.

Damien didn't tell me what was going on. He just stopped calling me. I still don't know why. I guess he found someone else. Turned straight or something. I was quite down, but hey. Life goes on. I continued working with Jim, but I just quit the partying. Couldn't be bothered with the scene.

I started drinking. I knew it wasn't a good idea, but in my head it was just one drink, y'know? I couldn't understand why people didn't want to feel like that all the time, and I would just have another and another. One night I became very drunk …

Jim drank a lot. He hadn't done before, but it became the regular thing to see him with a bottle of whisky. He'd have at least four of an evening, and he must've had more, but Margaret and I, we didn't see it. There was one evening he came home and broke open a new bottle of Scotch. He just poured himself glass after glass. Margaret was out with some friends, and she wasn't due home till just after nine.

I don't know what came over me. I drank. I had an entire bottle of whisky, and I sat there, speechless, until Maggie came back home. Andy must have phoned her or something; I can't really remember. She knew what I'd been doing, and she sat with me, asked me what was wrong. I couldn't tell her. I didn't have the courage. She yelled at me that I was a damned awful husband, and that if I couldn't trust her, who could I trust? I knew the answer to that, for sure.

Jim and Margaret had a huge row when she got home. She told him he was a lousy husband and that he never told her things any more. If he wasn't going to talk to her, he had to talk to someone. That someone happened to be me.

I wasn't thinking. I said to her that I would talk to Andy, and that if he wanted to tell her then he could. So I took him into the other room, and confessed everything. Right from the start, like I've just told you.

He told me he was in love with me. I wish he hadn't.

He told Margaret everything I'd said. I wish he hadn't.

Mandy Haggith

Dead Leaves

Dead leaves
float
underwater
like
memories, surfacing
only
when dragged
up
by the current.

Hailstorm

A hailstorm drummer strolls
to the spring tide shore,
mistakes our home for timpanum,
thumps till his fists are sore

then patters sticks across the water
so I start to feel I oughta dance.

He grins and picks up brushes,
loosens into jazzy swishes
fading to a gentle hiss
that lingers like the last dance kiss.

Mandy Haggith

Zen Gardener

wind on the loch
raking ruffled waves
into orderly white lines

Mark Ryan Smith

Harvest

(Note: A tushker is a long bladed tool used in Shetland for cutting peats.)

Screams, human screams, rattled in the ears of them all. Even above the wide, fearful roars of the wind, still the screams could be heard. And when someone heard a scream, it was difficult to discount the possibility that it had emerged from the hole in their own face. There were few words. Mostly screams. Terrible screams that were whirled away in all directions by the up and the down of the plunging ship.

Black rocks in front of black land topped with black sky. Swinging lights of ship and the rumbling, brutal white waves. The screams, so loud to those aboard, make no impression on the immensity of the night. The ship climbs, the sharp prow driving into the sky. She falls. She falls down the other side of the wrathful wave that has lifted her as easily as a child raising a doll from a toy pram.

There is one who does not scream. One whose noises are more than useless signifiers of the final acquiescence. One who throws out words of defiance. There is one – teetering in the bow, a length of rough twine balled about his wrist, lashing him hard to the rail – who curses and spits words of defiance at the fate that the wind and the water hurl him into.

His words will be heard.

Crew and passenger are made one by the storm. None of them, no matter how well-acquainted with the ocean, can keep their feet beneath themselves. Mothers arch over children. Men loop their arms around both. Objects clatter from shelves. Bottles and jars shatter against the walls of the cabin. Barrels, worked free from their places, vomit up their contents over the tortured, screaming boards.

And still and so on he of the prow does roar. See his mad words guided through the wildness of the night until softly they land on the ledge of a window. Tentatively his words explore the frame, feeling for a way through. They discover the tiniest fissure and in they creep, drawn, as if by a magnet, to the man who sits on the inside. Drawn, finally, to the man who sits. To the man who watches.

'They will all die tonight.' The breath that pushes out his syllables mists on the cold pane. His wife sees his inscrutable back as she moves silently over the stone floor. 'There is one that refuses. He shall be the last.'

His voice is toneless. Anodyne. The words no more than cold, pale echoes of his thoughts.

The ship see-saws sickeningly over the peaks of the waves. She is nothing. She is nothing to the wild, boiling, angry ocean. Bodies drop from the gunwales: they prefer the depths to the ship. No matter which choice they make, their end has been determined. No reprieve will be granted. No appeals will be heard. No angels will emerge.

The watcher pushes himself from his chair. His wife glances at him before turning her attention back to the stove. The thump of heavy boots leaps from the cold floor. The dog, uncommanded, follows him to the wind-rattled door.

'You'll mind about the supper.'

'Aye,' he replies.

The door opens and out he steps. The wind, enough to shock the faces of most, does no such thing to him. He closes the door behind the dog and turns his head to the crashing sea.

He sees the ship suspended on the point of a wave. There she sits as if hung from the sky, the water reaching up to lick her keel. This is how he sees her. Waiting. She is waiting for the next phase of her destruction. The invisible strings are snipped and she falls down the wave like a sledge down a snowy bank and explodes the waiting water with her bow. Lifting his tushker, he walks steadily towards the shore.

And the ship is pushed towards the shore. Not steadily. No. She tosses and falls and is thrown about insanely, but towards the shore she goes. And towards the shore he goes. He knows where she will strike. He has stood on the rock which she will strike. Many times he has stood there with the harsh land behind and the dark, unknowable ocean lying still and flat about him. He has learned this place. He has learned the lore of this place and, although he knew that this place was not his, he could nevertheless permit himself to think of it as his, due to his knowledge of its lore. And the ship was moving towards this place. Moving towards his place. Moving blindly towards his place.

She strikes! With an appalling crunch she strikes. And he of the prow is cart-wheeled over the rail as if he were no more than a puppet. His arm broken, he dangles heavy and can feel the fire depart him. He did not expect to be defeated so easily. The other passengers. He now sees, along the deck, the other passengers. They are far away. He wants to fall. He wants the twine to unwind itself from his ruined arm and permit his body to fall below. To the tearing rocks. To the black depths. To whatever it is that lies below. No more rage against the dying. No more resistance to the fading. He is approaching the silence. He is nearing the ease of the blackness of silence. No more smashing of the waves. No more of his terrible words. Only silence. No more of the screams. Silence. He can feel the silence. He can perceive it. Close to the silence. Reaching out. Reaching out for the final, enveloping silence.

A movement. Yanked away from the silence by a movement. By the movement of a shape. A shape and two colours. Black. Blacker than the black of night; and white, whiteness, placed against the blackness. Legs. Two legs. Then four legs. A head. The head of a creature. An animal. Then a dog. The man sees a dog, a white-and-black dog, from his one open eye. A dog has come to witness his ending. And a man. There is a man also. He carries something. A pole. A pole with a blade fixed to its end. Shouts. Shouts and cries from the deck of the rock-pinioned ship. Shouts for help. Shouts for mercy.

He climbs aboard. The deck is now an impossible gradient. People grasp at what they can but he walks unaided. A hand is held out to him. A desperate, quivering hand and a tiny, insignificant voice pleading to be the first one saved.

The heavy boot drives down the arm, flattening it against the deck. There is a moment of unbelief before the shock and the pain emerge. The man does not speak. The trapped forearm pinned beneath his boot. The hand twitching like a snared animal. The blade comes down.

Cut from the arm, the hand continues to twitch. The man raises his foot from the stump and takes life from its owner. Bending down, he carefully lifts the hand and drops it into his sack.

He is a practiced and efficient worker. Moving inevitably along the ship, he collects one hand from each being. His sack fills and the blood filters through the weave of the coarse cloth. Any attempts to resist are dealt with tidily and with great accuracy.

And he of the rail has witnessed all. He of the rail, unable to tear his arm free, unable to make himself not look, has seen the progression of the killing. He knows that his time is approaching.

The point of the blade jams into the wood at the side of his hand.

'You were the one who shouted defiance.'

The man at the rail could not answer. He had nothing left to say.

'You should not have acted as you did,' said the Harvester, softly. 'No angels are possible.'

Still he could not respond. He could not cry. He could not fight. He was less than numb. He could feel only his own impotence. He was nothing. He was, with his killer standing above him – cold, dead, unfeeling eyes staring down, his heavy boot upon the rail, his bloody fingers laced calmly in front of him – as nothing.

But he could also imagine that he was beginning to feel another thing. The tingle of another thing. In his guts and in his throat he could feel the beginnings of other things. Of words. He was going to be allowed some more words. He felt them move up his body. He felt his lips part and his mouth widen. He felt the words in his mouth. He felt his lips and his tongue move to make the sounds come out. He heard his mouth speak:

'Why do you hate so much?'

'Hate?' replied the Harvester, 'I do not hate. Hate is no more significant to me than love. I care nothing for either. Both are outside of me.'

Those were the final words the man heard before his body, arm still bound to the rail, dropped limply to the black water swirling below.

The Harvester, with great delicacy, sliced through the twine and removed the forearm from the rail. The blood ran warm over his hands. He lifted his head to the hill. His wife had the lamp burning. A beacon in the blackness to guide him home.

Daibhidh Martin

Black and White Noise

One day a young boy named Doug came across an old woman standing at the top of the track behind his house. It was more than three miles from the nearest village. He had noticed her monolithic silhouette and went to see if he could help her in any way.

When he stood next to her he saw that she was holding a photograph up to her ear.

She spoke in regular waves, not distracted, but nothing that she said made much sense. Her gaze was so distant that Doug thought she didn't even know he was there.

She threw her words out to the universe to determine on whose ears they should fall.

Doug tried to find out if she was okay or if she needed any help finding her way home. She just looked straight past him and said, 'You walk behind me and I will follow you home.'

Holding the photograph to her ear she walked without saying a word, but every so often would point a frail finger in the rough direction of the moon. Still he kept trying to talk to her, desperate to make sense of this, but she didn't respond.

He followed her to the shore and watched her walk peacefully until the water threw itself around her feet. She dropped the photograph and it came to rest on a clump of seaweed. Doug walked over and picked it up. He stared in confusion at a picture of a table on which the words *Eisd ri seo!* were inscribed.

As he held up the photograph to his ear he heard the woman begin to sing, 'This is the sound of the sea, come now and dance with me.'

[*Eisd ri seo* – Listen to this]

Thievery of the Ocean

It was a misty autumn night, the same year that George Orwell wrote *1984,* and four strangers were walking through a sleepy village on the Isle of Lewis. Their boat had run aground on the east coast of the island, due to the inhospitable weather and lack of a lighthouse.

They had been walking for about two hours without any sign of help and to make matters worse they were in desperate need of a drink.

About twenty yards down the road they came across a sign that read '*Taigh Ceilidh* ½ a Mile.' Now, not being local, they couldn't understand what was written, but with no real clue where they were they agreed that they had no choice but to follow the sign.

As they drew near they could hear wild noises and music. They reached the open door and looked inside, amazed at the sea of swirling bodies. Before they had even quenched their thirst they were linking arms with some local lassies. Drunk on the atmosphere and a little home brew, they didn't take long to understand.

Once the moonlight had faded they walked back towards their boat, carrying the tools needed to make it seaworthy again. As they rose over the last brow they caught sight of their stricken boat and began to run towards it. When they reached the boat they stopped and looked at each other, before proceeding to smash it into a million little islands.

As they stood there in a line watching the driftwood float away, all they could do was burst into fits of laughter as they started walking back to tell their tale about the unfortunate thievery of the ocean.

[*Taigh Ceilidh* – Ceilidh House]

Tiptoe

L ittle Hamish was eagerly rummaging around in the loft for any treasures that may have been left behind. His family had just moved into an old house in Back and he was desperate to find something interesting about the previous owners. Next to a pile of old berets was an empty cardboard box with a small notebook placed carefully on top. Hamish excitedly opened it to see what was written inside. The notebook was blank but an old, frayed sheet of paper, like part of a scroll, fell out. It was a letter that had been translated into English, from a language with dotted vowels, and slowly he began to read it out loud.

Dear friend,

I trust that this letter will find its way into the hands of one who will not ignore what it contains. For this is not a story drafted by the hands of a madman, but a man who has lived every word of it and can vouch for its truth. It is you that would be mad to ignore it.

I am a Viking man and fought many battles in my short life wielding a bloody spear. I tell you that the massacres, which I both witnessed and partook of, left such an indelible stain upon my mind that everything my eye encountered bore a vivid red tinge and haunted me to the point of delirium. It was in my frenzied state that I ran into a small man wearing no armour and little clothing. I fell on top of him and begged that he would take my spear and my life for all that I had taken in battle. He knelt beside me and whispered 'A man who has walked to the far side of the earth only has to stop and turn around to get home.'

I returned to my feet and felt his peace diffuse into my blood, eagerly running through my body. But what he said next I found truly amazing. I was momentarily paralysed in uncertainty about what to do. He looked intently into my eyes and, as he slipped a sheet of paper in my hand, said that the names of all the good people were written on the seabed.

I hastily made my way to the shore and began to climb the hill to get a clearer view of the seabed. The cerulean waters were moving softly and I was able to make out the names of my parents and some of my friends scratched upon the ocean floor. I stared intently until my eyes began to hurt but found no sign of my name. Distraught, I sat down and cried. As I loosened my grip on the spear for the first time, the sheet of paper I had forgotten about left my palm for the ground. Reaching over I picked it up and read, 'Wherever you stand, the North Star is still the North Star.' Leaving my spear behind I ran home to speak to my father.

Your friend
Ingimar

Hamish walked downstairs and, as he calmly put the letter on the kitchen table, told his mother: 'I found this in the loft. It's like a story Gran used to tell us, but I don't really understand it.'

Yvonne Gray

On the Ridge: Spring 2003

Sunlight glows on verdant slopes.
A tractor, crawling westward,
gules the greensward
quartering the land below.

Waves unfurl from the Atlantic
spume mantling sable rocks.
The falling sun blazons the ocean
with a shield of bronze light.

In the high fields
the black bull and the white bull
have tramped their borders for hours.

Head to head they stand
on the horizon now, breathing thunder
over darkening sky.

Yvonne Gray

Summer Terraces

At last the earth tilts back
and days ease into light.

Snow shrinks from stony faces;
springs of melt gush, tumbling

onto naked rock. Veins mesh
and green the swelling slopes.

In May grey skies turn harebell.
Blossom veils the orchards,

a bridal procession
lengthening round the fjord.

In July cherry trees are laden,
branches bending, jewelled in red.

Dwarf trees probe the soil
with grapnel roots. Branches gnarl

towards the mountainside,
thickened and twisted

in winters that clench
then ease their grip.

August comes and twiggy fingers
spurt hard green apples.

Alison Flett

Here He Comes

How different it would be if I was a bird. Oh, just think on that. Think how bonny from up there, the isle a darkling shape in a dark pulsating sea but a fair braw sight the night. The prinkling fairy lights of other folks' houses strung merrily over the braes and around the peakit shoreline, light and laughter spilling from open doors and *Happy New Years* ringing out like frosted bells in the clear night air. A special night. A celebration.

But then, when I travelled inshore, the lights winking farewell as I crested and dived up and over the braes, I would come to a darker place, the moor at the heart of the island.

The moor, with the dark braes all about.

I would hover high above it, my pale wings trembling like ghosts, but I would never see the croft. This croft where I'm now sat would never be seen, for its thatched roof would blend near seamless into the heather and peat bogs, like a patch of the same material on an old bit clout. And the wind, the reeving wind would rage here, blattering me sideways, shrieking me away out over the moor, skrecking and cawing, my screams swallowed up into the black maw of the night.

But instead I am here, sat in the croft, sat by the fire, waiting. Waiting, as always. I shiver and pull my knees up, hunkering deep into the wing-backed armchair.

Oh, but it's quietlike.

Just the crinkle of flames from the fire and the cries of the wind ricocheting off the inside of the lum. There's a puddle of light bleeding weakly from the wee lamp by the window, but further in the room is thick with the gloom of the night.

I sit forward and gawp into the fire till the darkness from outside creeps in about me, blurring the edges of my vision, and all I can see is the pointed tongues of flame lashing at the inner walls of the fireplace. There's a thick layer of stoor from many a long year of lashing, that thick and black now that the red brick of the wall has disappeared underneath it. My face, my face, I feel the burn of the fire on it, the jaggy heat prickling my flesh, but still I sit here gawping like a daftie, with an awful grue growing in my bones. My fingers grip the arms of the chair, the nails digging into the bare patches where the fabric has been scratched into cross-hatching. I keek down at my hands, at the whiteness of the bones showing through where the skin is stretched tight over my knuckles.

For Christ's sake.

It is madness, this waiting in the half-light with the fear fluttering at my thrapple, the awful ettling of what is surely to come. He is out there, I ken it fine. He is out there somewhere in the darkness.

He will come for me the night.

It is aye the same, this first night of the year, and lord knows why I am aye here waiting for it. If there was somewhere I could go and the bairns could come with me, my two bonny bairns in the bedroom through by. But there's nowhere to go, not really.

I hear a moaning and I ken this is it starting. It's starting now. There's a low moaning coming from somewhere outside.

Maaaaa

Maaaaa

The grue hotters in my bones and my fingers clutch at the arms of the chair. I ken fine what's coming and I cannot stop the dread reeving through me, though my very veins are clenched against it. After a while the moaning stops.

I leap to my feet, stride over to the kettle and flick the red switch, standing before it as it starts to boil. As I wait, I lean forwards over the sink, peering out the window, looking to see if he's there. All I can see is darkness and myself reflected in it.

The bump of the kettle switching itself off makes me jump. I take it over to the sink and pour the boiling water into the red plastic basin. Then I turn the cold water tap on full and wait as the pipes thud and groan. The tap retches a few times then splatters water into the basin. I reach for the washing-up liquid but stop when I hear a dull thud from outside. I stand frozen, my arm outstretched, waiting, eyes fastened tight on the window, ears straining to hear.

Nothing more.

I lift the washing-up bottle and squeeze a blob of bright green liquid into the basin, watching it froth and bubble under the jet from the tap.

I pick up a dirty plate and am about to plunge it into the soapy water when a noise from the window makes me look up.

Jesus!

I let out a scream and the plate slips from my soapy hands and slaps into the water splashing flecks of foam into my face. He's there, he's there, he's right there, his dark face glowering through the window, the black eyes flickering round the room and coming to rest on me, staring right into me with cold angry hatred. I just stand there, staring back, unable to move, until his face flips away into the darkness leaving just a square of black. The front door smashes open, smacking off the stone wall so that the house shudders and a cry of fright punches out of my mouth. I can hear the slow dunt dunt of heavy footsteps making their way along the flagged floor of the lobby towards the kitchen. I leap back as the door crashes in against the wall and the darkness of his large frame fills the hole it leaves. I look up at him and I'm trembling, my hands dripping soapsuds onto the scuffed and ripped linoleum. His shoulders heave up and down and the breath comes in noisy bursts out of his nostrils and he stares at me from under his thick black eyebrows before starting to move towards me. Shaking now, I am shaking, shaking as he bears down on me, but then just as I think he's away to grab aholt of me, he pushes past instead, breenging his way through the table and chairs to the armchair by the fire, my armchair. He bangs down into it, his arms hanging loosely over the sides and his legs pushed out in front of him.

I'm that feart and yet when I look at him I think, like I always think, that maybe I can make this different. Maybe it will be okay if I can only just be calm, act normal.

Any drink? he barks, and my heart gives a quick thump to my chest. It's always the first thing he says. My mouth opens and closes a few times as I look at the empty whisky bottle that lies on its side by the bucket. So dry, my mouth feels so dry, my tongue cleaving to the roof of it and sharp stinging tears gathering quietly behind my eyes.

Any drink? he barks again and I mumble No, no sorry, no whisky left. Will I make you a cup of tea?

What?! He turns slowly round to stare at me, one hand resting heavily on the worn arm of the chair. What's happened to all my whisky? Have you been fucking drinking it?

A tiny laugh screams in my throat. Oh come on now, I say softly, my hands fluttering round my neck. You ken I cannae stand the stuff. You drank it all yourself, afore you went out.

He stares at me and his breath is heavy and fierce. It's as if I can feel the force of it, blattering against me.

There was a good half bottle left when I went, he says, and if it wasn't you drank it, I want to ken who the fuck it was. His voice is getting louder, the words starting to ricochet inside my head. It was one of your fucking fancy men no doubt, come sniffing round soon as my back's turned.

No, no, of course not, I say, and I can feel my voice wavering. How could you say such a thing to me? It was your own self, like I said.

Are you calling me a liar! The words explode from his mouth and he leaps up out of the armchair, tumbling it over on the floor, its legs sticking awkwardly up in the air. There is a sudden roaring in my ears and the breath gasps out of me and I am scared, scared, so scared.

I don't think that's right, a wife calling her husband a liar. I don't think I can have that in my own home. He strides over to me, clattering through the furniture with the bigness of him. He grabs me under the chin, his fingers squeezing tight on either side of my mouth.

What do you say now? he asks, smiling at me. Are you going to say you're sorry?

I say nothing.

He gives my head a little shake with his hand. Come on now, he says, his teeth gritted into a grin. Say sorry like a good girl.

I stare past him at the wooden legs of the armchair all tapsalteerie before the fire. I stare past him and wait. I can feel the fear bubbling up inside me, gurgling in the back of my throat, but I can't say it. I want to say it, I want to put a stop to all this anger, all this bangstrie, but I can't. I just can't.

I wait with his breath warm in my face, stale alcohol and cigarettes. Another breath, his eyes drilling into me. Another breath. Another.

Finally I put my hand up to try and push his hand away but he grabs my wrist and twists me to the floor. I roll quickly onto all fours and start to scramble away from him but he catches hold of my ankles and drags me back. He swings his leg back and then forward, the heavy black boot hurtling into me between my legs. I scream and roll onto my side, doubled over, curling into the pain, oh god the pain, like a red hot poker being driven up inside me. I lie panting as the sharpness of the pain dulls to a deep throbbing ache. Then there is his boot again, thudding hard into my stomach, punching small grunts up out of my mouth, once, twice, three times. There's a moment's pause and then he bends over me, grabs a handful of my hair and wraps it around his wrist. I scream again as the roots are torn out of my scalp, then cover my mouth, remembering the bairns. He pulls me slowly across the floor like a carcass, pulling the weight of me by my hair. I reach for the upturned chair legs as he drags me past but they slip through my fingers. He pulls me on towards the door, then stops. He crouches down beside me, peering into my face, then he turns away from me, shaking his head.

An awful dree rises up inside me and I ken I have to get out. It's the only way to stop this. I watch the side of his head turned away from me and slowly creep my fingers round the edge of the door.

I feel sick, sick, sick.

I flip the door quickly open and try to wriggle to my feet, but his head snaps round and he dives towards me, pushing me back to the floor and sitting on my stomach so that my body is trapped in the kitchen and my head is sticking out the doorway on the cold flagstones of the lobby. I struggle frantically, arms flailing trying to push him away. He looks at me, then yanks my arms down, pinning them to my sides under his thick hefty thighs. He grabs hold of my ears and leans towards me, hot breath rushing from his nostrils. He's shaking, his face red.

Why do you do this to me? he says. Why do you make me so angry? He pulls at my ears, tugging my head round to face him. Fucking look at me when I'm talking to you! he shouts.

I stop struggling. I ken there's no point. I lie still beneath his weight and stare past him at the ceiling, at the black mould spots there.

Fucking look at me, will you! he says, lifting my head up and crashing it back against the floor.

I let out another scream as a flash of pain arrows across the top of my skull, then I shut my eyes and screw up my face.

He keeps on shouting, lifting my head up and crashing it back in time to the rhythm of his words. Will, you, do, what, you're, telt!

I screw my face tighter, trying to keep the hurt inside, not to let it out where the bairns will hear it. My head is a guddle of pain and fear and I can feel myself drifting, a blackening round the edges, and I think this is it, it's over, even though I ken it's not. Not yet.

He stops. He lets go of my ears. I breathe out, and open my eyes.

He's looking down at his hands, frowning. Och now, he says. What's all this about? His face suddenly crumples and tears topple from his eyes and spill down his cheeks. He bends his face into his hands and his whole body heaves up and down as he breathes the sobs in and out. I can feel the judders travelling through him and on into my own body. I'm sorry, he says. I'm sorry. I never mean to hurt you, really I dinnae. I just get so angry. So angry. And then you … I just don't ken what I'd do without you.

He reaches down and strokes the side of my head. I flinch away from his fingers, and my ribcage battles up, sinks down underneath him. Could you get off me please, I say. I cannae breathe properly.

He rolls one leg over the top of me and turns to sit with his back against the wall, his knees pulled up to his chest, greeting into his hands.

I stand up and for a wee minute I think of going to sit beside him, of trying to comfort him, but I want to see the bairns. I need to see them. I go quietly into their bedroom, pulling the door to behind me.

The two of them are sitting cooried up together on the oldest one's bed. They stare up at me as I come in, their wee fearty faces, their big fearty eyes. They're both greeting. I feel my own tears gurge up inside me but I swallow them back. I sit down on the bed and twine my way in between them, wrapping my arms about them, pulling them in close to me, trying to hush away all of their fright.

I sit on the bed and stare at the closed door, with the heat of their little bodies seeping into me. It is because of this moment I can never bring myself to leave, this precious moment alone with them. The feel of their wee shouders, their hands around my neck, every toty part of it. Cold and empty as I am, I feel the heat of them warming my bones. For just this single moment I go through all the rest, again and again, though it breaks my heart. It breaks my heart.

Any minute now he will come in. Any minute now he will come in with his gun, the same gun he uses for the rabbits. He will look at me with rivers running down his face, with seas, with oceans of sadness and time streaming out of him, and he will say I canna thole it any longer my love, this is the only way it can end. And I will open my mouth to say no, no, choose a different end, this is too awful, too awful, but all that will come out is the same thing that came out the first time and all the other times since. All that will come out is a scream. I will scream high and long and the scream will be a taut silver wire travelling out of me into eternity and the singing of the wire will call the bullet to me, spinning and whistling on its silver trajectory, spinning relentlessly on and on till it punctures my head and all the tiny fragments of me and my life and my memories are exploded into the air, and in just that fraction before I die, I will see it all so clearly. I will see him turn the gun around and place the barrel in his mouth, I will see my bonny bairns left alone in this godforsaken house with our two bloody bodies lying on the floor beside them, I will see all the many many things that could have stopped this from happening, everything that could have been said or done, all the times I could have left.

And maybe next time I will leave.

Maybe next year I will find the strength to end the endless repetition, to walk away from the house before he comes, to take the bairns and disappear into the blackness of the night, to set my soul free as a bird, send it skrecking and cawing into oblivion.

Maybe this will be the last time I hold them.

The very last time.

But shoosh now.

I hear his footsteps.

Here he comes.

Morag MacInnes

Herring Bones

This tractor tread in the mud
puts me in mind of
the herring bone lines
dovetailed in stone
on the way up to Marwick.
They push through the peat.

That ripple says, movement.
You
want to finger it, like
Fair Isle knitting,
like furrows in fields and on
Skaill when the sea ebbs. It says rhythm, it
talks about time. It's a kiss
that alters your landscape, soft
meeting hard.

It's in the bairns' hair when you
look for the parting, it's
like my stretchmarks.
It's all about shaping the space.
Somewhere there's
a Buckie quine
– hard hand in the fish spines and
one sharp knife.

Capstan Full Strength Navy Cut

She canna help it – pass a lighthouse, an she's off on
a ha'penny thing , to do wi
gruff men in jumpers, an sea boots cuffed
in oily wool. There's a tortoiseshell-lookin
wireless set: Hilversum, Luxembourg,
Bakelite knobs.
Plenty stairs, an brass
instruments, glass-tapped barometers
for strong thighs, an clever hands.

A tower worth Rapunzel. No posh princess up top, mind.
(Her Majesty's pinned downstairs
Next J I Shearer's calendar)
It's man stuff. Wind shiftin to the North an such.
Off watch, some tattie soup.
Capstan Full Strength, a pipe. Somebody
in the huff, combin his beard at the crossword.
An likely as kippers, or Robertson's jam,
disaster on the map.

Climb, log, an polish. They keep to routine.
If maybe some sea queen floats in,
sortin her hair wi a bit o' baleen, an
causes a swell in a shower of blankets
some nights – there's no comments. They just
tend an send
that bright blink through the weather. Message
to men. Watch the rocks. Avoid storms. We'll
keep you informed. Love, other men.

She sees heroes in towers,
red penknife reliable, droppin their darning,
to pull up some corpse from the ebb, an then,

Morag MacInnes

washed an toothbrushed
buttonin' jamas, punishin pillows an
waitin for one salty lady. Somebody tell the lass
that flash between fish, just before the big wave –
nowadays it's just electrics.
There's no big men loupin the stairs.

What Gets Said and What Gets Done

I want to tell you about this woman I met. She opened the door of a guest house in County Wexford, and the minute I saw her I knew I'd never forget her. There was something very still about her. At first I thought: how calm. Then I noticed how white her skin was. As if it hadn't been used much.

Did you want a room? she said. She was clearly thinking about something else.

Yes, I said. I'm just off the boat. I added the bit about the boat because I thought she needed time to snap into the conversation properly. Of course I was just off the boat, and I'd liked it. I was still feeling angry, but I was also excited.

(Doesn't everybody like sailing away? The treats – the food you wouldn't buy on land; the silly shop with its porcelain, cheap satin teardrop Pierrot dolls; sitting out pretending you know about wind direction and coastal shelves; putting sea between you and what you're stuck with most of the time?)

Ah. Well, you see, I have to ... she said. Then stopped.

I thought: strange, and I looked her over, like you do, for signs of mental decay, drink, degenerative disease.

She was immaculate. That skin, and smooth thin hair – black and grey in it, no dyes: she didn't look like a woman with any personal vanity of that kind. No. She looked as if she hadn't been unwrapped or aired at all. Like something just out of the box. She wasn't young, but she didn't look at all old. She was wearing a cardigan over a shirt, a beige skirt, and sensible busy person's sandals. Even her toes looked as if they hadn't done much work. Unscuffed.

Because I'd been angry I was hot all the time, my feet lathered in sweat. I felt at a disadvantage.

This was all happening, you must remember, in a split second. I thought: Lady of Shalott, Rapunzel, the girl in the Rumpelstiltskin story.

The reason I picked her guest house was because it struck me as odd. I like to think I'm odd. Not very; just glancingly. I pick such places to stay in because, paradoxically, I expect to meet people like me. There's a foolish thing, now. I'm different! Are you different too? Excellent, let's get together.

This house had piles of shells outside, brought up from the beach by grateful guests. Lots of different kinds; some quite big. The garden was full of plants I associated with the Mediterranean, and there were wee birds darting in and out of the wide shiny green leaves. It reminded me of Barcelona, where I'd been very happy watching parrots flying through pineapple trees in the middle of the traffic. I suppose I thought: here's a place like a place where I was happy – perhaps something will rub off.

You see, the thing of it is, she began again, Micheal's dead this morning, and I have to go to the undertakers' at two, but I'll give you the key and you can make yourself at home and have a cup of something and directly I'm back I'll get the sheets for your room.

She stopped again, and then said: it's been a shock. He does everything, the running of it all.

Then, after another stop, she said: he just dropped down like that.

I'll find another place, I said; I wouldn't dream of putting you to the trouble. I'm so sorry.

No no no, she said. It's no problem at all if you don't mind me just popping out. I'll turn the sign. Come in out of the rain, come on now.

There were more shells inside; books about geology, dried seaweed, sea urchins. You would think she was trying to bring the whole beach in bit by bit. She had classical music playing. She'd been hoovering to it, before I rang her bell.

A long thin room doubled as hall and breakfast room. There were wall-to-wall windows – the view was just stunning. Sea, sky, raindrops on the double-glazing. Suddenly a seagull would shoot by, vertical or horizontal, depending on which wind was blowing it. You couldn't see the beach from the windows, because the house was stuck right on the edge of a steep cliff. There was a gate at the end of the garden, then about a hundred steps straight down. All you could see, right along the length of the room, was sea and sky. But you couldn't hear anything at all from outside, just her classical radio station playing from the kitchen. That made it seem a bit unnerving, like watching an action film with a music score but no words.

I saw the house from the ferry; I marked it out then for a place that had seen some weather in its time.

She gave me a great big wooden key ring.

Micheal made them because the guests keep losing them, she said. Which I'd guessed.

There's the kitchen.

It was terrifically neat but dark, like a German kitchen. It had that heavy wooden look, over-endowed with knobs and curls. I thought I saw Micheal's hand in it. A coffee cup, saucer and spoon sat on the table, very neatly placed. She hadn't looked like a mug person from the start. I was pleased to be proved right.

And here's your room. It's got the view too.

A tasteful room, but she was embarrassed because last night's linen was still on the floor in a heap. Her plastic bucket of cleaners and mirror polishers was on the bed.

If you just leave your case, I'll have it perfect the minute I get back. Oh, and if you hear the television, don't you worry: it's my daughter. She's ... we're all a bit shocked, still.

It's a terrible thing to lose a father, I said.

I can't tell you how matter-of-fact, and yet dazed, she sounded. It was like talking to somebody sleepwalking.

It's my father. My dadda. Her granddaddy, Micheal is. I'll tell you all about it, but I just have to be off now.

She put on a green anorak; checked her handbag, looked at herself in the mirror.

Sure I look like a ghost now, don't I, for heaven's sakes? she said.

She hadn't switched the radio off, and I didn't like to touch it myself. The Irish accent sounded very foreign. It reminded me I was here to have a holiday. Then I remembered that, though I called it a holiday, it was really like beginning a new, very demanding job. I had to learn to enjoy my own company. I had to learn to stand on my own two feet instead of lolling about on a man as if he was a sofa. There were a lot of things I had to practise in order to keep on track.

So I took the guide book out of my suitcase and began to tick off interesting places round the coast. A deserted lighthouse, a seabird colony, a cloth museum. Tick, tick.

Won't you just sit like family and make yourself comfy while I finish the room? she said. She had been away a full hour and a half. I had time to make a lot of ticks and some notes, too, and I felt a bit easier in myself. So I said:

I tell you what, I'll sit on the dressing table chair. Did you get your business done?

Why you're a Scot! I only just noticed. It's a lovely burr. Yes, but it's the money that's the thing, you know, with the casket and all. They won't be wanting any old rubbish for dadda. Did the phone ring? It's never stopped, once the word got round.

I didn't hear it, I said.

Then she got busy making the bed. What I noticed was that she talked as if I were a doctor or a priest. She said: I do my own linen normally but the tumbler drier went, you see, and the launderette is closed all day Wednesday. Micheal said he could fix the drier but I knew he couldn't. He got the back off it and all, and then my second sister, that's Iris, she called and asked for him to go down and pick up her babbies from the school. She doesn't get on with her boss; doesn't get on with anyone. She's what you call the black sheep in this family. You know how all families have black sheep.

This distracted me for a second. She noticed right away that I wasn't up there with her.

You know, all families, sure they do, she said.

I had been thinking, I don't know your first name. You don't know mine either. I haven't signed the book. I think I'm the black sheep in my family, for walking out on a good man, a comfortable man who can grout and fix the dimmer switches on lights.

But I switched back to concentrating right away. I could see she was sharp about being paid attention to.

Well, he won't let her pick up the babbies, though it's ten minutes out of her time that's all. He says she's a skiver. Well, she is a skiver; we've never got on and she went and married an Englishman that didn't stay. There's not a lot to do here in the winter, you see, when the visitors are gone. You need to be bred to a place like this. It's all hotels and guesthouses: busy as you like then all boarded up and the bosses in Tenerife and the dregs just left sitting painting the skirting boards.

So Micheal went like the soft bugger he is. He would always do anything for her, anything for his own girl, though I knew he wasn't feeling too good. There was sweat on him: you would have thought it was roasting out, when it was just like this foul old rain and wind. So he never got there: he just dropped down. And me stuck with the dirty laundry and bookings phoning in and no fresh breads.

All this while the sheets are flicked out, starched and airy; the lemony duvet cover slides up the clean plump duvet; the television remote gets a polish; the birds sport about soundlessly in the soaking wet shiny Mediterranean plants beyond the double-glazing.

And we're a big family, you see.

She stops. Another thing to think about.

I'll have to get myself organised about the food. And the drinks. But anyway – so Mrs Clifden phones the ambulance because it's her doorstep he's dead on. That took forever. It's some way, you know, and the road's very wet – we've had such a deal of rain, I hope it won't spoil your stay – but you see, he was dead anyway. She was a nurse, so she knew. Come to that, she saw her husband drop the same way. Now that's bad luck if you like, isn't it.

That's maybe a blessing, I said. A quick death. You might not think it now, but – you don't want to linger, in pain.

It seems okay to say this. It seems okay to say anything. It's like talking in space, floating about free.

I don't want to linger in pain, I think. One big wallop and gone. Much better.

She knows I've slipped off her story, and looks sharp.

A blessing for him, maybe. What about me? she says. Stupid fella. He was heading for it, my dadda. He was always up to something, some wheeze. This place and another one across the bay he maintained, and he did maintenance work for the big hotels, you know: the chains. They were always after him. I used to say: my dadda, you'll kill yourself with pleasing other people. You should sit a while. I told him and told him. He said: I sit when I'm fishing. That's my sitting time …

So it's Micheal in the pictures all along the breakfast room, with the fish he caught. Cups and weighing machines and local newspaper headlines scissored out and framed, I think – then stop myself and pay attention.

… but it was everything for Iris and she's an idle piece. She'd been a worry to him because … well, I can see you're a married woman yourself so you'll know. The minute the Englishman was out the door she had another fella on the go and then another. My dadda said great God above, Iris: it's no way to behave. Can you not see the pain you're putting me through? That's what he said: the pain you're putting me through. You're just like your mother before you, he said to her. He said, why can't you sit content like your good sister here and mind the houses? You don't see her putting herself about Wexford painted up like the Whore of Babylon, do you? he said. So they had been at it fighting nights. He was under a lot of stress. Our name, you know. We have a name in this town.

She looked at me, then hoisted up the Hoover in one hand. That's me, you see: the good sister, she said.

What happened to your husband? I asked. I meant, after that, to ask what was so bad about her mother. I was lining up questions. In between all this talk, you understand, she was showing me how to get the channels on Irish TV, putting a lavender sachet on the pillow, fetching me soap and moisturiser, a little throwaway shower cap with *Welcome* written on it.

Ah, he ran off with a girl called Heather. She had red leather trousers. Nobody ever dreamed of leather trousers around here, but after she came they were all over the town like a rash. It was a sexual thing. He just wanted a lot of sex and I couldn't be doing with it, do you know how it is? Sure, once in a while it was fine, but not night after night when I had all the work to be getting up to. That was seven years ago, so Anna Maria doesn't remember her dadda: Micheal was her real dadda, though she called him grandaddy.

You don't look like a leather trouser person, I said, and she let out a high sound somewhere between a spit and a chuckle.

No, I wouldn't be seen dead in them, she said. It's not a thing to be missing and regretting and fretting over, a man that can have his head turned by a pair of leather trousers. There we are now, all nice and fresh. Will you be wanting a meal tonight?

Oh no, I said.

I do seafood, she said. I'm very popular. It'll be open as usual.

She paused, thinking, frowning; then shrugged.

I suppose we will. I will. We're in the guide book, for the meals.

Then she said, in the same breath almost: you know, I don't just know what I'm going to do without him. I don't just know. In the kitchen and all. I hadn't thought about that.

You've got the family, I said.

Oh, yes, I do. But they don't take anything to do with this business. He was everything, around here. It was all his thing. It was all done for my dadda. Look here – and she picked up an ornament – he made all my shells into these little fellas like goblin kinds of things, and had them sitting in among the shamrocks. In the winter nights. He did them with superglue and then painted them up. There's hundreds of them. I put them on the windowsills. He used to put them in the shops for sale, too. And you see the writing on the bottom?

A Present From Ireland, in wavering italics.

And the talk out of him! I like to stay in the background. I suppose that'll change.

I had planned to walk on the beach; go to an Irish supermarket, for the foreignness, then maybe picnic in my room with the bird-and-sea view and the strange television. On the way out to explore, I picked up the visitor's book. It was full of glowing comments about Micheal's hospitality. Great craic! someone had written. We were up all night laughing with his stories. A real character.

The beach was stony, but there was a shell line where the tide had turned. I picked up a couple of cowries and augers with pink whorls, and one hobnail–shaped shell with a blue line running through deep brown.

In the supermarket I found the kind of food that might attract visitors – soda bread and black pudding and speciality jams. I got potato scones, white cheese – but I had no knife, fork and spoon set neat in their plastic jacket, ready for such picnic emergencies. And I didn't have a glove compartment full of salts, peppers and vinegars from motorway cafés all over Europe any more, either. I reminded myself to think harder from now on; to pay attention for myself. When I got back up the cliff to the shell house, the notice had been turned round again. *Vacancies!* it said.

In Ireland in summer, the dawn comes early. I heard her get up, rouse the child and feed her cereal in front of the TV.

She put her music on. I took my guide book into the breakfast lounge.

The rain was streaming down, all the pampas grass tossing around like hair.

I could see her moving about in Micheal's kitchen as she cooked me the full Irish. She was probably humming bits of Bach.

The coffee was real, and in a big pot. The food seemed pleased with itself, as though it had been cooked by someone who got carried away by tastes and smells. Suddenly I remembered leaning over a balcony in Spain and smelling horses and lemons, all mixed up. I remembered Eiskaffee, in Bremen, and carp with green bones. I remembered basil, and the smell of nasi goreng in the Turkish stalls in the back streets of Cologne. I remembered how those things tasted and smelled to me, almost as if I was in those places. I realised I didn't feel angry, but hungry.

This looks lovely, I said.

It's a pleasure, she replied. But she was just going through the motions, talking over me at the view. I wondered if she remembered blurting it all out yesterday, at all. She looked like someone who had been out all night in a deep dark crackling Arctic winter. I could tell that she felt as if her whole body was too stiff to move. I could tell that she couldn't smell anything at all, though it was all perfectly, perfectly cooked. Such was her desperation, her awful grief. Out in the gale the birds were ducking and diving. It looked like a bit of a battle, keeping abreast of that wind, but you couldn't hear a thing beyond the Bach, so it was hard to tell whether it was a Force 9 or not.

I ate up every scrap of her lovely, crisp full breakfast.

It was a terrible night of rain, she said, while I was paying. Where are you going from here?

I'm going to visit Sterne's birthplace, I said. I always liked Sterne. My husband never did.

That'll be the bad road, I'm afraid, she said. We're not too hot on our roads.

I wanted to put something meaningful in the visitor's book, to show we had shared Micheal's death day – maybe say: Maura looked after me so well in difficult circumstances, or something like that. But we were never introduced. Maura was the first name on the business card that she gave me along with my receipt, in case I wanted to recommend her to some other traveller. But I didn't feel I could use it without her permission.

A safe journey, now! she said at the door, with the music and the fishing pictures behind her and the grasses tossing.

I hope so, I said, and I laid the shells I'd gathered under the wall where the wind wouldn't scatter them, in case I came by her place again some time.

Robert Davidson

F111 Over Culloden

Phrases such as 'the dead are sleeping' roll
over the battlefield now as cannon blast and smoke
did then. Thankfully the notion of 'glorious'
has never been applied to these boys, or their deaths.

Over there is where the British ordnance lined up.
Right here is where the Highlanders stood and took it.
I don't have a personal axe to grind, as likely to have
ancestors on one side as the other; more likely both.

We know the result, though. We *are* the result,
or one of them, of progressive union through war.
Now, from nowhere, comes a sleek fighter, pointed,
low over the battlefield and deafeningly loud and

all at once they are up again, clamouring and clinging,
frightened and tearful in their tattered grave-clothes,
their dark, stricken eyes. The commotion they make,
it's going to take ages to get them back down.

Eva Faber

Something Perfect In Between

My parents would roar and screech at each other. My mother was dragged by the hair screaming, then punched and jumped on till she vomited blood. My father was scratched; my mother broke his glasses with a swipe, she listed his shortcomings in a voice thick with tears. After that, they didn't sleep together. My mother would creep into my single bed and sleep with her feet on my pillow; my father retreated sulkily to his part of the house.

Soon afterwards, my father announced he was buying a beach umbrella. A red and white, super-deluxe beach umbrella.

The sheer scale of it was astonishing. When my parents prised it open in the lounge it filled most of the room. Its metal spokes arched above us like the ribs of a giant animal. The light bulb in the centre of the ceiling shone faintly through the canvas like a distant star.

On the next hot day, we drove to the beach. My parents left me outside the changing rooms, guarding the umbrella. It lay flat on the grass, aimed at the crowded beach. I tried to look as fearsome as my polka dot swimsuit would allow. A breeze carried the smell of the sea and sunblock lotion. I sniffed and waited. My parents emerged from opposite ends of the changing rooms: my mother in a black bikini, my father in a pair of trunks in the style of Tarzan.

My parents carried the umbrella onto the foreshore like a couple of lifeguards. I ran along behind. The scorching sand slipped under my feet. We had to find an empty spot in the midst of all those stripy towels and deckchairs and parasols. Nothing approached the dimensions of our umbrella. My father squinted at the panorama to find a space good enough for us. 'Over there,' he said. We followed him to a less populated part of the beach. He opened the umbrella with his powerful arms. It creaked as he did so. My mother and I watched as he hauled it upright and screwed it into the ground, secure and firm.

The circle of shade was immense: enough for a family with ten children, but my parents only had me. It was a miniature new country we'd discovered, round and ridged with sand. I put my arms out and spun around inside its borders like a drunken seagull. My parents applauded and laughed. My father made jokes about the principality of Liechtenstein and buried half a dozen cans of beer where the sun couldn't get to them. He'd have them later. We stood around looking at distant swimmers, small specks bobbing up and down in choppy water. The umbrella towered above us, absorbing the heat and the light. Soon the sand was cool enough for us to spread our blanket and stretch out. My mother posed in her snappy two-piece: it showed off her delicate rib cage and the swell of her hips.

'You're an attractive woman,' said my father.

My mother snorted and spooned out potato salad from a tub. Our Fanta fizzed in our plastic cups. We ate and drank; the warm salt air made me tired. After eating, my mother and I fell asleep, lying side by side with all the room in the world to spread our limbs.

But the sea was creeping in closer and the shade was running away from us. My father woke us a few times to shift the umbrella. We migrated to different parts of the beach, following my father's path through all the prostrate bodies on the sand and then lying down as soon as the blanket was ready in our new location. Each time, our umbrella was erected for us anew. It swayed a little in the breeze. I felt at home again as soon as I looked up into its red and white segments glowing in the sun.

All this work made my father thirsty. He began to dig holes to look for his beer. He couldn't remember where he buried it. My mother laughed.

'You're behaving like a dog, Alfons.'

My father dug faster. He was leaving molehills all over the beach.

I began work on a sandcastle. I didn't want to go swimming. The sea scared me; even in the shallows children whose names I didn't know played rough, pushing and shoving, dunking each other in the waves.

My father went for a dip; my mother went back to sleep.

When my father came back, he just stood there and admired my mother. She was still lying in the shade of our umbrella: it cast a soft light on her limbs. My father told her she was looking 'exquisite.' I don't think she heard him. My sandcastle was growing bigger with extra turrets and thick walls.

But the swim had made my father thirstier still. He was trying to figure out all our previous geographical locations. He began to dig trenches. He burrowed like a madman.

My mother said, 'Stop, Alfons. Stop right now.'

'Mia, this is the last time, I promise. I think we started off over there…'

And he dug his final trench – a long ditch in between a couple of young ladies who were sunbathing in their deckchairs.

'Excuse me, I have put my beer somewhere in the underground,' he said as he dug up a spray of sand that landed on their feet.

My mother said it was only a matter of time before he got arrested.

In the afternoon the breeze stiffened, turned nasty. We were all together on our blanket again, stretched out under our umbrella. Sand blew into our mouths and crunched between our teeth. A steady stream of people filed past us on their way home. We ignored them and stared up at our canvas sky.

And then something dreadful happened.

A gust of wind uprooted our umbrella, flinging it into the air with explosive force. It landed on its side and then it sped away, twirling along the shore. It had sharp spikes on both ends – one silver, the other one crumbed and sharper still.

The red and white animal made its way down the beach. It was equally at home in the air as on land, alternating between the two. It would fly a short distance before diving towards the ground with a peculiar violence. It would spin along the beach at great speed before becoming airborne again. There were screams, the crowd parting in the umbrella's path as if a shark had appeared in the shallows.

My mother yelled: 'Alfons, do something! Someone will get killed!'

My father ran after the umbrella and flung himself at it. There was a battle between man and metal and canvas. He fought with the thing bravely as the wind threatened to carry them both off into the hot sky. In the end, he threw himself on top of it and held it down. A swift grab at its inner parts and the umbrella was closed. The beast was subdued.

My parents got dressed standing up on the beach. They put their clothes directly on top of their bathing suits. I said goodbye to my sandcastle. It had survived the wind. My shame-faced parents hauled the umbrella away.

It swung between them at knee level rather than riding triumphantly on their shoulders. It oozed wet sand. My father's forehead was gashed.

By the time we got to our car one of my father's eyes was swelling shut. My mother cried out, 'Alfons, you're hurt!' as she slid into the front seat beside him and began to dab at his injuries with a chamois we kept in the glove box.

That evening my mother handed me a small pack of colouring pencils and a piece of blank paper before disappearing with my father into the other bedroom. Soon my parents were murmuring to each other rather than shouting.

'Mia, you're still a beautiful woman.'

'Alfons, don't be ridiculous! *Alfons.*'

I wondered if I should keep standing outside their door in case I was needed.

'Mia, don't stop.'

My father's voice had never sounded that way before.

I was hanging about in my room, waiting to be put to bed. And for my mother to join me, even if I had to squash up with my nose against the wall. But the house had gone quiet.

I laid out my pencils and paper. I drew the beach umbrella. I gave it carefully delineated segments. I coloured the red in. For white, I just let the paper show through. The umbrella was standing upright in a beach full of yellow dots of sand. No-one came to tell me to stop, so I added a sandcastle which was yellow as well. With six turrets. And inside each one I drew a cylinder in brown: the six unopened tins of beer I'd dug up and built my castle around. I used the blue pencil to make a big sky and then lay down in my clothes to have a rest.

Hours passed. I became hungry and my thoughts turned to the potato salad we'd had on the beach. It had just the right amount of mayonnaise.

No-one came to see how I was.

Somewhere in the middle of the night I remembered an ocean liner, slowly making its way across the horizon. I switched on the light and added the ship to my picture. I outlined it in black and didn't colour it in except for some red and brown splotches that were meant to be rust. The boat that had carried my parents to Australia might have looked like that. They told me it had rusty port-holes.

Just before dawn, I realized there was something missing from my drawing: the sea. I recalled the colour of the water – neither green nor blue but something perfect in between. It was the best colour I had ever seen. I wondered how I could show this on the paper.

There were only six pencils in my set.

Laureen Johnson

Mainlanded

I come on a rushing train,
quiet as a church tonight.
As light leans westerly
we gently leave the sea –
a shadow of itself,
pale edging boundary –
head into the heart of land

through dull-gold harvest baled and stubbled;
great alien fields and still-green trees
thick-leaved and shady. The horizon's lost,
the world's rim, swallowed up in hills
and further hills, and harbours are unknown.
I come alone

towards the lurking dark,
to ground on concrete, waiting
for a wave.

Sharon Blackie

Freefall

'Golf Delta Charlie, cleared for takeoff.'

The voice in my ear startles, piercing the cocoon of unreality in which I've wrapped myself. The sounds and smells of the cockpit jerk back into consciousness; once again I'm aware of your presence beside me. Unusually silent. Are you ready to go? I can't see your face but I can picture it clearly – that same old small smile, one thin dark eyebrow tilted in amusement. Judging me. Testing. *Come on, Cat – jump. Let's see what you're made of. Look – the other children can do it. Why can't you?* Oh, but don't worry, Mother – I'm really not going to lose my nerve.

'Cleared for takeoff, Golf Delta Charlie.' My voice cracks and my mouth is dry, but this time around it's not from fear. I know that you don't quite believe it yet, but I've mostly dealt with the fear.

A firm push of the throttle and the engine begins to roar. We're moving forward slowly now; we cross the line at the beginning of the runway and we are in a place of transition. But once we reach takeoff speed, throttle fully open – once I pull the yoke towards me and lift up the nose – well, then: we're committed. There is no turning back: we are quite out of choices. We move on and move upwards, or we crash, and the chances are that we die.

And there it goes again: that same old flutter in my stomach as the small Cessna lifts herself gently from the runway. Yes, we're leaving the ground now – and do you see how it is? How all that's familiar – all that's known and understood – falls away there beneath us as we hurl ourselves recklessly into this clear blue void. The world shifts and tilts as we bank to the south and turn out of the airport traffic pattern. Look down below you, now – what do you see? It's no longer the earth that you know. It fades, deconstructs itself into two-dimensional patterns: a patchwork in fabrics of blues and greens. Quilting lines cross it in straight lines and curves, the stitching uneven and puckered.

'Golf Delta Charlie, clearing the zone en route.'

'Golf Delta Charlie, roger. Have a good flight.'

Communication ends with a decisive click. We're on our own now; we're heading out west and there's no-one out there to talk to even if we wanted to. But we were on our own for so long, you and I. *You and me against the world*, you used to sing. In the days before it became you and me against each other. And so here we are again – just the two of us, tightly strapped into the confined world of this tiny cockpit. Together again – now, when I finally get to show you that I've learned how to fly. And who would have believed it? That, against all the odds, I would learn how to fly.

We take our position on the narrow strip of asphalt that marks the boundary between the earth and the relentlessly blue Arizona sky. I shake my head but no-one is watching; I am slick with sweat, horrified to my very bones. The beautiful all-American giant of an instructor next to me murmurs soothingly between instructions and explanations. I cannot believe I'm doing this. We are rising now, rising and I'm trying not to look as the earth slips away beneath me and a chasm opens up in the place where my stomach should be. Eyes fixed to the instrument panel as though, if I turn away, the airplane will dissolve around us, leaving no other choice than freefall through the unforgiving desert sky. Holding the yoke in a death-grip, knowing for certain that if I let go or even loosen my hold we'll plummet to the ground. I am holding us aloft by sheer force of will, risking an occasional glance at the horizon to be certain that our wings are level. But then we're turning and isn't the nose too high? – and the wings are dipping and I know we're going to fall, to slide, to just slip down in a beautiful graceful dive, because how can it be possible that the air supports us so? How do we dare presume?

But then we're level again and he takes his hands off his yoke. He turns to me and smiles, blue desert skies shining out of his eyes, all space and distance and glory. 'Hey,' he says. 'You're flying.'

Do you see how far I ran that time? All the way to Arizona. Do you see, all those years, how I measured my progress in the distance I placed between us? Ah, but all that I was, I chose to become in complete opposition to you. Because it's a strong, tight cord that binds us together. And some connections can't be broken, no matter how hard you try.

You never could have imagined that I'd learn to fly. Come on now – be honest. No, I really didn't think so. *Oh, Catriona*, you'd grumble, your post-box red lips thin and pursed with irritation. *You're such a fearful child. You're afraid of your own shadow.* Ah but feel it now – feel it. There's no shadow up here. Feel the clarity, feel the lightness as it all falls away.

Do you remember when you tried once to teach me to swim? You had medals for life-saving: a wall of certificates to attest to your courage and success. You wanted me so badly to follow in your footsteps. *The first thing you do is to learn how to float. And then you'll be able to swim.* But I couldn't float, could I? I was always so afraid. If I let go of my hold I would fall through the water – slip down, insubstantial, and sink to the bottom like a displaced stone. *Just breathe now,* you told me. *Just breathe, just relax. There's really nothing to it: it feels just like flying. I'm here, little Cat. I won't let you fall.*

But I knew perfectly well that no human could fly. And even with your arms thin but strong underneath me, I was far too afraid to try. Because how could I be sure that you'd be there to catch me? How could I know that you wouldn't let go?

Such a perfect day. Do you see the firth down there below us? The water strangely becalmed after the night's wind and rain; sea in the distance merging with sky. Everything so very still. And you – you're so quiet over there; you seem quite relaxed. It's a morning worth relaxing into: on a blue sky day like this you can see clear into forever. The mountains shimmer in the morning sun, hovering in the distance like a mirage. Currents of air rush by, tumbling around the propeller, slipping under and over the wings, constantly shifting, ever-changing. For a little while longer there's nothing to be done; nothing that will stop me from basking in the healing solitude of these high places.

Nothing, except for you.

Nothing, except for your voice. With me all the time; egging me on to failure.

My feet are ready over the rudder pedals, tense. My arms are rigid as I clasp the yoke, and concentration screams in my brain. Pull the power out: feel the plane slow. Pull back the yoke: watch the nose rise. Oh, dear God – I can't do this. I can't.

But I have to do it. You have to stall the plane so you can learn how to recover from it. Then if it happens by mistake you'll know what to do. You'll be safe. Come on now, concentrate. The nose is way too high

*but don't stop now, Cat – don't you give up. Let it happen. For once in
your life, let it happen. The body of the plane shudders and I feel it all the
way through my shoulder blades and still I pull back and any moment
now ... Just don't think about it. The buffeting intensifies, stronger now,
stronger – keep pulling back and then we'll stall and the nose will drop
sharply and the wing will fall off to one side ...*

...And if I screw it up we'll spin.

Come on, scaredy-Cat! What are you frightened of? Jump, why
don't you?

*Ah, no. No, I can't do this. It's bad enough trusting my instructor
to do it; it's another thing entirely to do it myself. What if I press the
wrong rudder pedal? And what if I press the correct rudder pedal but I
don't do it quickly enough? What if we spin? What if we fall?*

Scaredy-Cat!

No, no. No. The stakes are too high.

I let out a shaky breath. 'I'm sorry,' I tell him. 'I can't.'

I can't.

*I'm so very high up here, and the water seems such a long way down. I
can hear your voice there below me, urging me on.* Come on, Cat, get
it over with – just jump. *But I don't want to jump: I know what'll
happen if I jump. I'll crash and I'll break myself on the hard flat surface
of that glittering blue pool. The bouncy little diving board down below
for once looks like a haven – I'm way, way above it here. Ten steps I had
to climb to reach the first platform, and there are ten more up to the
highest stage of all. Ice-cold fingers creep around my neck and squeeze
and let go, squeeze and let go, over and over again. My heart is pounding
a deep bass rhythm and a grizzly bear is crushing my rib-cage in a death
grip. I can't do this. I don't want to do this. The world begins to dissolve
around me as my breathing quickens and my eyes lose their focus.* Oh,
for God's sake, Cat – what's the matter with you? Are you going
to stay up there all day? *Your voice startles me and I sway a little.*
Cat? *I close my eyes for a moment – ah, that's better. No more cold hard
water, just a soft blissful darkness.* Cat! What are you doing, Cat?
*And then I feel it – slipping away, everything slipping away as I sway
and I tumble and I feel myself falling but it's such a blissful feeling and
so very easy to let yourself go ... And for a moment – just for one blissful
moment – it feels as if I'm flying.*

And then something crashes into the side of my face.

*And the last thing I see is a beautiful red jellyfish swimming away
from my head, swimming out into the water, growing, expanding and
it's so very pretty ...*

So tell me – what do you think of it up here? No, it's not like being in
a passenger plane at all. Just close your eyes now – breathe it all in. The
smell of the cockpit: vinyl seats, dusty electrics, the acrid engine odour
of burnt oil and old friction. The constant drone of the engine, the
rhythmic thrum of the propeller. The morning sun fragmenting through
a web of small scratches on the Perspex windscreen, a kaleidoscope of
yellow and blue light.

You always loved planes, didn't you? Sunday afternoons watching
the old war movies on TV – *Battle of Britain,* and *The Dambusters.* They
were your heroes, you always said. *Pilots: think how much courage they must
have, Cat. To hover all the way up there, in those tiny, flimsy machines. Can you
imagine how much courage it must take to fly like that? Taking their lives into their
own hands.* So does it make you happy now, to be flying with me? Did I
finally make you happy? I never was too skilled at that. Perhaps a better
daughter might have succeeded, but I never could seem to do enough
for you. So many ways I found to disappoint you. *For heaven's sake, Cat
– smile, can't you? Oh, Cat – don't you have any emotions at all? Why won't you
play, like normal children? Just let go, Cat – let go.* And sometimes I would
think about the children you lost – about the babies that never were
born. And I'd find myself wondering if, somewhere among those lost
children, there might have been the daughter you wanted.

I know what you're thinking – that I'm talking crazy. But you were
the crazy one; I was the rock. You – ah, but you had no fear. You threw
back your head and your red shoes glittered and you laughed and you
swung and you danced. You danced, and it seemed that you would never
stop. *You're so wooden, Cat. Relax, why can't you? Just close your eyes and let go.*

Let go. Time after time, you said it. You said it that day when I slipped
off the platform and gashed my face on the side of the diving board.
But I wouldn't cry. Not once. Not once on the journey to the hospital;
not once as the doctor put the stitches into my cheek. *Let go,* you said,
your face flushed and hectic, eyes brimming with anger. *For God's sake,
Cat – just let go now, and cry.*

But I knew what happened when you let go.

Sharon Blackie

I know what to expect when I come home from school and see the light already shining in the long, empty hall. You are home from work early; that means only one thing. A tight knot begins to form in the pit of my stomach. Quietly now I slip to the living room door; slowly I peer in. I hold myself tightly, muscles tense and ready for flight.

You're pretty far gone. Half-sitting, half-lying in the wing chair by the gas fire, skirt hitched up around your hips, blouse crumpled and stained. You must have been at it for hours. The bottle of Bell's is open and half-empty on the table beside you – you don't bother any more with the fiction of pouring it out of the teapot. Your eyes are closed, your mouth loose and slack as you mumble along with Shirley Bassey. A House is Not a Home. My mouth twists in a sad little reflection of your customary irony. Dark blue shadows lurk under your eyes, your complexion like old uncooked pastry. I bite the inside of my cheek as a stray sob escapes from your mouth and wonder how it is possible to love so much and yet hate so much at the same time. Your tears flow freely now; thin colourless snot escapes from your nostrils and collects in a pool at the corner of your mouth.

I turn away before you can see me: I know what will happen if I stay. You'll turn all your misery back onto me. You'll carp and you'll criticise; you'll pick at me and dissect me. And I'll shrink back inside and squeeze myself up like a plasticine ball and I'll make it so small that one of these days I won't be able to find it again. Upstairs in my room I lie on my bed, trembling. I try to swallow, but something is stuck in my throat and I can't catch my breath. I can't seem to breathe in properly, and even when I do, I can't breathe out again.

From time to time I hear a crash downstairs; at every noise I flinch.

See the mountains stretching out there ahead of us, hard triangular edges protruding through the mist? See how they come into focus – see how they change from misty monochrome to full, glorious colour as we approach them? They're so very different from the mountains in Arizona. There are trees here – geometric strips of forestry land stretching out like great furry caterpillars. And there's water – lochans scattered like pieces of broken mirror, reflecting the sky. Look down there now, as the earth slips away beneath us. See how it curves and bubbles and flows, raising itself up to the sky as it spreads on out to the west. The Native Americans say that the earth is the body of the Great Mother. You can see her shape down there, they say: you can see her form. The curves and the contours, the hard lines and jutting bones. And, looking down below us now, it is easy to see what they mean. Look over there: a small circular breast rises to the north, crowned with a swollen nipple; the burns and the gullies burrow like wrinkles deep into her aging skin. They say that Mother Earth lies on her back and opens herself to the embrace of Father Sky. That she endures everything, as women have always endured.

There's no fear in your face as you look up at him; there's not a trace of resignation. I'm too young to know what it is that shines from your eyes and gives him a moment's pause for thought, but looking back at the memory later I will see that it is a cold, hard will to endure.

You close your eyes as the first blow falls on your unprotected chest, but then you open them again and you look right at him. It only seems to make him madder; his jaw clenches tightly and his face gets even redder than it already is. Can't you see that you're just making him madder? The spasms begin to take hold of my throat again and I have difficulty swallowing the saliva that's building up in my mouth. Calm, Cat, calm. Breathe quietly, now, or he'll hear you. But I've held my breath for too long and I'm starting to feel dizzy. Another blow, and still your eyes are fixed on his face, steady, unwavering. What are you looking at, you stuck-up bitch? he yells, and lands a blow on the side of your jaw. A grunt forces its way out of your mouth, but you won't cry out. And all the time, you simply look at him. With every blow that falls you look right into his eyes and with every blow that falls I gasp for a breath that will not come and the blows become weaker and weaker and his breathing becomes more and more ragged – until eventually the blows cease. And as he turns and walks out of the room I see that my Daddy is crying.

The next morning you wrest me from my sleep when it's still dark; Daddy must only just have gone out fishing. You carry me downstairs and sit me at the kitchen table and give me a bowl of hot sweet porridge. As you run up and down the stairs throwing clothes into the suitcase that sits by the kitchen door you explain to me quite calmly that we're leaving and we're not coming back. But where are we going, Mummy? I ask. I don't know, little Cat, you say. And you run a gentle hand across my cheek and you smile. I don't know, but we'll find somewhere. I'll look after you. Just you and me, sweetheart. You and me against the world.

We're right in the heart of the mountains now, and looking down into ink-blot lochs so clear that you can almost see the brown trout playing on the bottom. Isn't it beautiful? Don't you just love it here? Well, you must do, I suppose. I guess that's why you came back here after all those years – back to this wild Northwest Highland shore where you began your life as a married woman. What was it that brought you back to this, of all places, at the twilight time of your life? An echo, maybe, of simple tranquillity; of incandescent skies and heather-coated mountains and shimmering seas. Maybe you were looking for peace, at last – a place where you might finally find the clarity that you need to break through the murk that's enshrouded so much of your life.

And me? All those years, I carried the fear with me. Afraid to fly. Because you let go of me after all, didn't you? – and I spiralled downwards into a place so deep inside of myself that I never could begin to find my way out. Always so calm on the surface, always so controlled. Always so afraid to let go. What changed? Well, I'll tell you what changed. I was diagnosed with panic attacks. Me. Cool, calm Cat. Competent Cat, senior corporate lawyer Cat. Always in control Cat. Diagnosed with panic attacks and advised to see a psychiatrist. Ah, no – not me. I was never the crazy one: I was always the rock.

I didn't go to see a psychiatrist: I learned how to fly. I learned how to fly and at forty years old it's my turn to be crazy now. To put my trust in a two-seater can with a couple of flimsy wings attached and an engine that looks no more complex than that of the average lawnmower. Do you see what I'm saying? Just look at it out there: at the unchanging immensity of the clear, empty sky. We are surrounded by blue; we are bathed in it, steeped in it. Perfect cerulean blue. Blue pervades every pore of my skin. I can feel it: I can almost taste it. Ripe lime with a bouquet of ozone, tangy on the tongue and cool on the skin. Do you see now what I'm doing? I am becoming a creature of cold blue air. I am immunising myself against the earth and all that would weigh me down.

But look over there – a solitary raincloud. It floats in the sunlight, just like a mirage. Shall we fly on towards it? Shall we fly, you and I, as we've so often done in the past? *Cat,* you would say, your face drawn and suffering. *I don't understand why you're always so angry with me.* Yes, the sky ahead is changing now, as it so easily does on this west Highland shore.

And sooner or later the blue will transform to the colour of ashes as storm-clouds build up in the west.

A sudden sharp gust of wind and oh, dear God – what's happening now? No – no, it's okay. There's no need to jump: it's just a little turbulence as we pass through the mountains. Just a little shudder, just a small drop of the nose. It startled me, that's all. You needn't worry: I'm quite in control. I've always been in control, haven't I?

One of us had to be.

Just another gust of wind, that's all it is – slithering under her belly and nudging up her nose – ah, but that's too high now, the airspeed is beginning to fall – press the yoke forward again, lower the nose. No, that's not sweat on my brow – I'm past all that, now. I got my license, remember? I learned how to fly. Nothing you can do now will change that – nothing you can say. *Scaredy-Cat! Why won't you jump?* Another sudden jolt; the turbulence increasing in intensity now. Do you want to be on the ground? It just isn't an option: there's nowhere out here we could land. Everything's fine, now, I'm doing just fine. Nothing is going to paralyse me now – not even the memory of you dancing in your red shoes, red shoes carrying you away into the dark forest and never stopping, just dancing on and on and out of control…

Ah, but this isn't good, is it? Skittering around from side to side as if someone has us dangling on a string. Here's the root of the problem: whatever immunity we think we have from Mother Earth is an illusion. And even the sky can turn on you, with raging gusts that batter you and shake you, and threaten to dislodge you from your precarious perch six thousand feet above the ground. Another sharp jolt from below then we're sinking; my breath catches in my throat and my head bumps against the ceiling of the plane. And that same old talon claws at my stomach and those same cold hands creep around my throat and begin to squeeze … Can you stop it now, Mother? Can you stop me from falling?

Above us a large bird tumbles, searching for a thermal. A buzzard, maybe even a golden eagle – I can't tell from here. But she's still up there. She's struggling, but she's still up there. And the image slips into my mind like a stream of cool, clear water.

Eagle Woman.

It had been such a spectacular flight to Sedona: my first cross-country solo flight. I walked into town to stretch my legs before heading home.

And there, through the window of an art shop, I spotted a print. Against a golden background of rock and sky, a woman knelt on the edge of a cliff. She held a drinking vessel before her, as if in the form of an offering: maybe even supplication. Superimposed over the figure of the woman was another figure – with the same shape and attitude, but with the wings and the head of an eagle.

It was a painting of transformation. Woman transforming herself into eagle.

I went into the shop and looked more closely; the title of the print was *Eagle Woman.* The woman behind the counter told me she'd always admired it. 'Looks like a Native American angel, doesn't she? Looks like she's just thinking about maybe jumping off that cliff and testing out those wings for the very first time.' She smiled at me: a smile of feminine conspiracy. 'Guess we all know how she feels, hey, hon?' Her face softened and her eyes became sad for a moment. 'Trouble is, most of us just turn right around and walk on back down that mountain. We're all too scared to fly. After all, who's going to catch us if we fall?'

And in the warm flush of success that accompanied another milestone in my flying career, I wanted to say to her – No. Don't you see? That's not how it's supposed to be. Listen, I wanted to tell her: listen. We learn to save ourselves. We learn to fly under our own steam, and we make our own safety nets. We card and we spin and we wind – and we weave. From our hopes and our dreams we weave ourselves back into life. From our hopes and our dreams and the fragile gossamer threads of our courage.

'Two November Romeo, ready for takeoff on six. First solo.'

First solo. All by myself in this tiny plane. There's no-one else here to stand between me and death: it's just me. It's all down to me. A large black crow steps onto the runway and stops, eyes fixed on the small white plane. Looking directly at me; challenging me. I return her gaze; I look down the runway and I look into the eyes of my fear. But for the first time in my life I do not run away from it: I stand and I stare it directly in the face. I meet it head-on and I find it a poor, scrawny creature that lurks in dark places and feeds off carrion. The crow turns away; flaps her wings and flies off across the field. So many things on the edge of my consciousness, ready to fall into place. But I don't have time for them now: I don't have time to think. I'm too busy doing the one thing that I

knew I couldn't ever do. I'm surrendering; I'm preparing to fly.
'Two November Romeo, cleared for takeoff.' Just as they've said so
many times before. 'And good luck, hon.'
I smile slightly as I push in the throttle and hurtle down the runway.
It is a moment of perfect purity: I am calm, I am clear; I am flying.

I close my eyes and gather those threads around me now. I shut you
out and I steady my breathing and relax my grip on the control wheel.
I wipe the dripping sweat from my brow and follow the dancing steps
of the plane. Where she leads, I follow. I follow with eagle eyes: eyes
that see to the front and the side, seeing through the past and beyond
it into the future. The future: sharp and clear, unfolding before me in
perfect Technicolor. I stretch out my arms, and I fly.

I fly, and I save the only life that I can save.

Here we are, now: we're through. Leaving the mountains behind us,
emerging into this cool, green valley where you've made your home. The
air is calm again now, and a ray of sunlight breaks through the clouds
out west. And, finally – do you see? – this is what it is about. Learning
to let go of all the old fears, all the old patterns. Because there is no
room for them in the sky. Flying demands a perfect, pure concentration.
If you slip, you fall. If you panic, you die. And so you focus with all
your strength and with all your will and with all your heart. You keep
yourself in the sky by the sheer power of your belief that you can,
and in the purity of this focus you begin to lose sight of all that might
previously have held you back. You let the old life slowly begin to melt
away. And the process of transformation that ensues is redolent of
an old, old alchemy. Just look around you – everything is so simple up
here. You balance on a knife-edge, but it's a clear, clean cut, and what
bleeds away is doubt.

The letter arrived on a Saturday morning. I recognised the handwriting,
of course, as it lay face up on the floor by the door. I recognised it from
some distance and stood quite still, watching and waiting. Waiting for
something – I don't know what. But I was right to be afraid of what was
inside. It was cancer, you told me, and it seemed you were dying.

I am eight years old and my mummy is dead. She's lying on the sofa so

155

pale and still and I can't wake her up no matter how hard I try. Tears trickle down my face even though I'm a good girl and good girls don't cry. But I'm alone in the house with her, it's the middle of the night, and it's dark – so dark. I'm frightened; I'm not feeling well and my mummy smells funny and she won't wake up. I swallow hard; I can't cry. I have to be brave and take care of her. I take a deep breath and I swallow my tears and ignore the strange spasms in my throat. I sit down beside her and I keep watch till morning; I hold off the demons alone.

So many small deaths, over the years. I thought I had mourned the loss of you years ago. And now I don't know whether I'm crying for you or for myself; for the years that I suffered you or for a future that's empty of you. Because who will I measure myself against now? Because I have loved you as fiercely as I have raged at you.

Because no other love can compete.

Do you see the house now, over there on the brae? The whitewashed stone walls gleam white in the last golden rays before the rain clouds come to veil the face of the sun. It's time, now: it's time. We're over the loch and I'm flying as low as I dare. I pull back the power and slow us right down, then reach out and open the window by my side. Air rushes into the cabin; I can't hear you any more over the whistle of the wind. I take the paper bag from the seat beside me – yes, I know: it's not quite as elegant as the urn, but the window will only open a crack. I open the bag and I shake out the contents. The wind takes you: a pale brown stream of ashes drifts down and settles on the surface of the water like sea-foam. The bag remains for a moment, flutters wildly against the palm of my hand like the wings of a captive bird.

I let go.

About the Authors

Pam Beasant, originally from Glasgow, now lives and works in Stromness, Orkney. She has been published widely as a poet and has written many information books for children. In 2006, her play, *A Hamnavoe Man*, was performed at the St Magnus Festival. Her biographical study of Orcadian artist Stanley Cursiter will be published later this year, and she is working on the final edit of her first novel and a libretto for an opera in collaboration with composer Gemma McGregor. In January 2007, Pam was appointed as the first George Mackay Brown Writing Fellow.

Sharon Blackie is a chartered psychologist specialising in creative imagination techniques and storytelling. She is a published writer of non-fiction and short fiction, and she is currently completing both an MA in Creative Writing and her first novel, which is loosely based on her story *Freefall*. She splits her time between a croft on the shores of Loch Broom by Ullapool, and a cottage in Cummingston, on the Moray coast. Sharon is a partner in Two Ravens Press.

Robert Davidson is the author of two collections, *The Bird & The Monkey* and *Total Immersion*, and editor of a third, *After the Watergaw*. His book length poem, *Columba*, was published in *Poetry Scotland*, and performed both on radio and as a drama. *Dunbeath Water – an Oratorio* was performed three times during Highland Festival 2003, and again at Nairn Arts and Book Festival 2007. He was Editor of *Northwords* magazine and *Sandstone Review* and is Managing Editor of Sandstone Press Ltd. His next book will be *Shadow Behind the Sun*, written with Remzije Sherifi.

Angus Dunn is the author of *Writing in the Sand*, a novel published by Luath Press in October 2006. Many of his short stories and poems also have been published. He was awarded the 1995 Robert Louis Stevenson Prize and the 2002 Neil Gunn Short Story prize. Angus is from the Highlands of Scotland. He has been known to wear a kilt, but does not speak Gaelic.

Eva Faber was born in Australia and has lived in the Scottish Highlands since 1993. She won the Neil Gunn Award for her fiction in 1994 and has been published in various magazines since then, although most of her energies have been channelled into teaching and parenting. She is also a photographer and painter.

Alison Flett was born and bred in Edinburgh but has been living in Orkney for the past eight years. She recently won the Belmont prize for children's poetry and was shortlisted for the 2004 Scotsman/Orange short story award. Her collection of poetry, *Whit Lassyz Ur Inty* (Argyll Press, 2005) was shortlisted for the Saltire First Book of the Year Award. She has just been awarded a SAC grant to work on a book of short stories about island life.

John Glenday is the author of two full-length collections: *The Apple Ghost* (Peterloo Poets, 1989) won a Scottish Arts Council Book Award, and *Undark* (Peterloo Poets, 1995) was a Poetry Book Society Recommendation. In 1990/91 he was appointed Scottish/Canadian Exchange Fellow, based at the University of Alberta and in 2000/2001 he was Associate Writer at Edinburgh University's Centre for Lifelong Learning. Poems have appeared in numerous anthologies, most recently *New British Poetry* (Graywolf Press, 2004) and *100 Favourite Scottish Poems* (Luath Press, 2006). He lives in Cawdor, and currently works as a coordinator for addictions with NHS Highland.

Clio Gray was born in Yorkshire, brought up in Devon and has been living in Scotland for the past fifteen years, where she works at her local library. She has won many prizes for her short stories, most notably the Scotsman/Orange Award in 2006. Her first novel, *Guardians of the Key*, a historical mystery, was published by Headline in 2006; the sequel, *The Roaring of the Labyrinth*, will be published in August 2007. A collection of short stories, *Types of Everlasting Rest*, is published by Two Ravens Press in July 2007.

Yvonne Gray lives near Stromness in Orkney. She teaches English part time and is also a musician. Her poems have appeared in various magazines including *Cenrastus*, *New Writing Scotland* and *Poetry Scotland*. She was Featured Poet in *Northwords 33* and in *Sandstone Review 3*. Other publications include *Rationed Air* (with artist Carol Dunbar), *Swappan the*

Mallimacks (Galdragon Press) and *Nouster* (Braga Press). She received a
SAC Writers' Bursary in 2002.

Andrew Greig is the author of six collections of poetry, the latest of
which is *This Life, This Life: New and Selected Poems,* published by Bloodaxe
Books. His five novels are *That Summer, Electric Brae, The Return of John
McNab, When They Lay Bare* and *In Another Light.* His latest work of non-
fiction is *Preferred Lies.* He lives in Peebles and Orkney.

Nicky Guthrie was born in Edinburgh, brought up in Glasgow and has
lived in the Highlands for the last twenty years. She has an MA in English
Language and Literature and, more recently, achieved a distinction in the
Open University Level Two Creative Writing Course. Many years ago
she won a poetry competition and a short story competition; she has
since had a number of pieces published in various magazines. Inspired
by her time working at the Moniack Mhor Creative Writing Centre, she
now hopes to devote more time to her writing.

Mandy Haggith first studied Philosophy and Mathematics and
then Artificial Intelligence and spent years struggling to write elegant
computer programs that could help to save the planet. A decade ago she
left academia to pursue a life of writing and revolution, and has since
travelled all over the world researching forests and the people dependent
on them and campaigning for their protection. In 2003, she returned to
Glasgow University to study for an MPhil in Creative Writing, gaining
a distinction. A pamphlet of her poetry, *letting light in,* was published in
2005. Her first full-length collection, *Castings,* is published by Two Ravens
Press in April 2007. She lives on a woodland croft in Assynt.

Morag Henderson grew up in Culloden. She left the Highlands when
she was seventeen and went on to live in a variety of different places,
including Glasgow, Edinburgh, Galashiels, France and Nova Scotia,
Canada. Eventually she came home to Inverness, where she currently
lives and works. She has had stories and articles published both in Canada
and Scotland, most recently in the magazines *The Leopard* and *Random
Acts of Writing.*

Elyse Jamieson is 14 years old and lives in the South Mainland of

160

Shetland. She has previously been *Shetland Young Writer of the Year* for her age group, and more recently was 'highly commended' in the *Royal Commonwealth Society Essay* competition. She hopes to become a journalist in the future.

Laureen Johnson is from Shetland. She has written plays, poems and short stories, a local history book and a short novel, *Shetland Black* (2002). Her work appears in the *New Shetlander* magazine, and has also appeared in various other Scottish publications. A selection of her dialect poems is soon to be published by Hansel Co-operative Press.

David Knowles studied philosophy and physics at Oxford. He is an RAF pilot flying Tornados out of Lossiemouth. When not deployed overseas, he splits his time between a cottage in Cummingston, on the Moray coast, and a croft on the shores of Loch Broom by Ullapool. David is a partner in Two Ravens Press.

Anne Macleod lives on the Black Isle and works as a dermatologist. Published work includes two volumes of poetry and two novels – *The Dark Ship* (Neil Wilson Publishing) and *The Blue Moon Book* (Luath). She is currently working on her third novel.

Kevin MacNeil is a novelist, poet and playwright from Lewis. His books include *Love and Zen in the Outer Hebrides* (Canongate) and *The Stornoway Way* (Penguin). He has held writing residencies in Scotland, Sweden and Bavaria.

John McGill was born in Glasgow and now lives in Orkney. He has taught English all over the place and has published a collection of short stories, *That Rubens Guy*, and a novel, *Giraffes*. His stories have featured in a number of anthologies and have been broadcast on BBC Radio 4 and Radio Scotland.

Morag MacInnes is Orcadian. She's a writer, lecturer and community artist whose work has appeared in various Scottish anthologies. Her story *The Scotswoman's Pillowbook* was an Asham Award winner in 2004 and her poem *Here Lives a Painter* was commended in the first Wigtown Poetry Competition in 2006.

Daibhidh Martin is twenty-five and was born and raised on the Isle of Lewis. He studied English Literature at Strathclyde University and has now returned to Lewis to write full-time. He writes fiction and poetry in both English and Gaelic. He also performs his work alongside musician Iain Morrison and has performed at various venues including the CCA in Glasgow, The Arches as part of Celtic Connections and on the Tom Morton show on Radio Scotland. He is currently involved in a writing residency on the Isle of Harris.

Donald S. Murray is from Ness, Isle of Lewis and currently lives and teaches in Shetland. A widely published writer, his short story collection *Special Deliverance* was shortlisted for a Saltire Award and his poetry has also been anthologised and shortlisted for national awards. His latest book *Speak To Us, Catriona* is about to be published by the Islands Book Trust.

Alison Napier was born in Fife but has spent most of her life in the Highlands. She has an honours degree in Sociology from Aberdeen University and a Diploma in Social Work from Bristol Polytechnic. She lives in Sutherland with her partner Lynda and currently works part-time as a social worker for a local authority in the fields of mental health and old age. She is working on her first novel.

Pauline Prior-Pitt is a poet and performer living on North Uist. In *Waiting Women, Addresses & Dreams, Ironing with Sue Lawley,* and *Three Score Years &Some,* she writes humorously and seriously about ordinary things that affect women's lives. Her poems about North Uist appear in *Storm Biscuits,* and in *North Uist Sea Poems,* which won the 2006 Callum Macdonald award. Pauline has read her poems on BBC Radio 4, on Channel 4 and Central television. She has appeared in festivals all over the country.

Joanna Ramsey has lived in Orkney since 1988. A small collection of her poetry, *Walking on Hay,* and two poetry pamphlets have been published by Galdragon Press. Her short stories have appeared in *Chapman, Northwords, Cutting Teeth* and other magazines. In 2000 she was awarded a Scottish Arts Council bursary, and was a prizewinner in a short story competition run by *Good Housekeeping* magazine. She lives in

Stromness with her daughter, and is writing a book about her friendship with George Mackay Brown. She also works as a freelance copy-editor for a London publisher, and makes ends meet by cleaning houses.

Cynthia Rogerson is a Californian, living near Dingwall. Her first novel, *Upstairs in the Tent*, was published by Headline Review in 2001. Her short stories and poems have been short-listed in various competitions and included in anthologies and literary magazines, as well as broadcast by the BBC. Her second novel, *Love Letters from my Death-bed*, is published by Two Ravens Press in April 2007. She has four children, an ex-husband in her extension, a very tolerant boyfriend, and some hens.

David Ross took a degree at Edinburgh University and then stayed on in the capital for another fifteen years, working at a variety of jobs ranging from lecturer to dish-washer. He wrote two draft novels and ran a Creative Writing workshop for *Theatre Workshop* as well as playing and song-writing in several bands, including *Poetry Roadshow*, a words/music fusion of performance poets and musicians. Returning to his home town of Tain, he began writing his short story collection, *Highland Views*, which will be published by Two Ravens Press in April 2007. He now works as a guitar, composition and recording tutor.

Mark Ryan Smith is thirty years old and is from Shetland. He has lived both in Glasgow and Edinburgh but is now happily ensconced in the isles with his wife and baby daughter. He has had various jobs, including electrical engineer, plumber's mate and building site labourer. He currently works in the Shetland Archives. He has published both poetry and prose and, in 2005, was awarded third prize in the annual McCash prize for Scots poetry, a competition run jointly by the *Herald* newspaper and Glasgow University.

Peter Urpeth lives and works on the Isle of Lewis, Outer Hebrides. His first novel, *Far Inland* was published by Birlinn Polygon in April 2006. His poetry has been published in *Northwords, Cencrastus* and other journals. He is the Writing Development Coordinator for HI~Arts, the arts development agency for the Highlands and Islands of Scotland. *www.farinland.net*

Copyright Information

Fiction from Two Ravens Press

Love Letters from my Death-bed
Cynthia Rogerson

There's something very strange going on in Fairfax, California. Joe Johnson is on the hunt for dying people while his wife stares into space and flies land on her nose; the Snelling kids fester in a hippie backwater and pretend that they haven't just killed their grandfather; and Morag, multi-bigamist from the Scottish Highlands, makes some rash decisions when diagnosed with terminal cancer by Manuel – who may or may not be a doctor. Meanwhile, the ghost of Consuela threads her way through all the stories, oblivious to the ever-watching Connie – who sees everything from the attic of the Gentle Valleys Hospice. Cynthia Rogerson's second novel is a funny and life-affirming tale about the courage to love in the face of death.

'Witty, wise and on occasions laugh-aloud funny. A tonic for all those concerned with living more fully while we can.' **Andrew Greig**
'Her writing has a lovely spirit to it, an appealing mixture of the spiky and the warm.' **Michel Faber**

£8.99. ISBN 978-1-906120-00-9. Published April 2007.

Nightingale
Peter Dorward

On the second of August 1980, at 1pm, a bomb placed under a chair in the second class waiting room of the international railway station in Bologna exploded, resulting in the deaths of eighty-five people. Despite indictments and arrests, no convictions were ever secured. Exactly a year before the bombing, a young British couple disembarked at the station and walked into town. He – pale-blue eyes, white collarless shirt, baggy green army surplus trousers – and twenty yards behind him, the woman whom, in a couple of years he will marry, then eventually abandon. He is Don, she is Julia. Within twenty-four hours she'll leave for home, and he will wander into a bar called the *Nightingale* – and a labyrinthine world of extreme politics and terrorism. More than twenty years later their daughter Rosie, as naïve as her father was before her, will return to the city, and both Don – and his past – will follow...

'Nightingale is a gripping and intelligent novel; it takes an unsentimental and vivid look at the lives of a small group of Italian terrorists and the naive Scottish musician who finds himself in their midst in Bologna in 1980. Full of authentic detail and texture, Nightingale is written with clarity and precision. Peter Dorward tells this tragic story with huge confidence and verve.' **Kate Pullinger**

£9.99. ISBN 978-1-906120-09-2. Published September 2007.

Parties
Tom Lappin

Gordon yearns for power; Richard wishes reality could match the romantic ideal of a perfect pop song; Grainne wants life to be a little more like Tolstoy. Beatrice looks on and tries to chronicle the disappointment of a generation measuring the years to the end of the century in parties. *Parties*, the début novel by journalist Tom Lappin, is a scathing, insightful and profoundly human commentary on party politics and the corrupting effects of power. But above all it is a satire: a black comedy about young people getting older, and learning to be careful what they wish for, lest they end up finding it.

'Compelling and absorbing: the story of five friends growing up in the '80s and '90s, through the voyage from idealism to disillusion that was left-wing party politics through the turn of the century.'
Paul Torday (author of **Salmon Fishing in the Yemen**)
£9.99. ISBN 978-1-906120-11-5. Published October 2007.

The Most Glorified Strip of Bunting
John McGill

The US North Polar expedition of 1871-73 was a disaster-strewn adventure that counts amongst the most bizarre and exciting in the annals of Arctic exploration. *The Most Glorified Strip of Bunting* is a fictionalised account of its events, based on the firsthand accounts of the participants. A recurring theme of the novel is the clash of two civilisations – Inuit and European – and the mutual misunderstanding and hostility that arise from it.
£9.99. ISBN 978-1-906120-12-2. Published November 2007.

Prince Rupert's Teardrop
Lisa Glass

Mary undresses and wades into the boating lake. She dives and opens her eyes. In the blur, she perceives the outline of a head – she reaches... A dead bird. But she will keep searching. Because Mary's mother, Meghranoush – a ninety-four year-old survivor of the genocide of Armenians by the Turkish army early in the twentieth century – has vanished. Mary is already known to the police: a serial telephoner, a reporter of wrongdoing, a nuisance. Her doctor talks of mental illness. But what has happened is not just inside her head. A trail of glass birds mocks her. A silver thimble shines at the riverbed – a thimble that belonged to her mother. A glassblower burns a body in a furnace and uses the ash to colour a vase. Rumours circulate of a monster stalking the women of Plymouth. Has her mother simply left – trying to escape the ghosts of genocide in her mind – or has she been abducted? It is left to this most unreliable and unpredictable of daughters to try to find her, in this moving, lyrical, and very powerful work.

'Lisa Glass writes with dazzling linguistic exuberance and a fearless imagination.' **R.N. Morris**
£9.99. ISBN 978-1-906120-15-3. Published November 2007.

Short Fiction from Two Ravens Press

Highland Views
David Ross

Military jets exercise over Loch Eye as a seer struggles to remember his vision; the honeymoon is over for workers down at the Nigg yard, and an English incomer leads the fight for independence both for Scotland and for herself... This debut collection of stories provides an original perspective on the Highlands, subtly addressing the unique combination of old and new influences that operate today.

'I'm a big fan. A fine organic collection that advances a viewpoint, culture and history quite other than the urban central belt that still lopsidedly dominates recent Scottish literature.' **Andrew Greig**

'A view of the Highlands with a strong element of political and social comment. Ross explores these concerns in convincingly human terms through the lives of his characters.' **Brian McCabe**

£7.99. ISBN 978-1-906120-05-4. Published April 2007.

Types of Everlasting Rest
by Scotsman-Orange Prize winner Clio Gray

From Italy and Russia in the time of Napoleon to the fate of Boy Scouts in Czechoslovakia during the Second World War, Clio Gray's short stories are filled with intrigue, conspiracy and murder. Laden with sumptuous detail, each story leads the reader directly into the compelling and sometimes bizarre inner worlds of her fascinating characters.

'Clio Gray is a master of atmosphere and sensuousness. She combines historical realism with the bizarre, whimsy with the macabre. Reading her is like being at a sumptuous feast in a palace, just before it is stormed.' **Alan Bissett**

£8.99. ISBN 978-1-906120-04-7. Published July 2007.

Poetry from Two Ravens Press

Castings: by Mandy Haggith.
£8.99. ISBN 978-1-906120-01-6. Published April 2007.
Leaving the Nest: by Dorothy Baird.
£8.99. ISBN 978-1-906120-06-1. Published July 2007.
The Zig Zag Woman: by Maggie Sawkins.
£8.99. ISBN 978-1-906120-08-5. Published September 2007.
In a Room Darkened: by Kevin Williamson.
£8.99. ISBN 978-1-906120-07-8. Published October 2007.

Available direct from the publishers at
www.tworavenspress.com
or through any good bookshop.